THE IRISH RECITER

Edited by
Niall Toibin

THE
BLACKSTAFF
PRESS

BELFAST

First published in 1986 by
The Blackstaff Press Limited
3 Galway Park, Dundonald, Belfast BT16 0AN, Northern Ireland

Reprinted with corrections 1987, 1990, 1992, 1996

Printed by The Guernsey Press Company Limited

British Library Cataloguing in Publication Data
The Irish reciter.
1. English poetry — Irish authors
I. Toibin, Niall
821'.008'09415   PR8851

ISBN 0-85640-369-5

CONTENTS

FOREWORD

Compiling an anthology is a thing to be undertaken lightly or not at all. Deep thought on the implications of each selection could frighten off the most assured. What could be simpler than to marshal half-a-hundred of your favourite ballads, poems and recitations? There is much happiness in ransacking the archives and rummaging through the memory for the source of some half-remembered couplet or oft-quoted snatch of verse like 'Up the airy mountain, Down the rushy glen', or 'She only smiled – O'Driscoll's child – she thought of Baltimore.' It is a joyous chase but fraught with frustration, for personal taste affects not just one's perception of the intrinsic merit of a piece, which may not even be a relevant consideration in this case, but of its 'rating' in the rolling opinion poll that is the folk tradition. Agonies of indecision attend the proposed inclusion of what had seemed an obvious choice. Do I really love it for its humour and sheer performability rather than its political sentiments? In this, as in less reputable areas of behaviour, the only practical policy is 'never apologise, never explain'. I can but try to describe the process which led to the final assemblage.

I was guided primarily by remembered recitation rather than by reading. Val Vousden's broadcasts of more than forty years ago and Eamonn Keane's regular spot on Radio Éireann's *Take the Floor*, which transmuted, yet continued, the tradition of the *seanchaí*, suggested many items. I called also on recollections of blushing aunts and slurring uncles at Christmas parties, wakes and weddings, scurrying through inaudible renderings of 'He's gone to school, Wee Hughie', or bellowing above the Shannon's roar: '"Break down the bridge!" – Six warriors rushed. . .'

At first I was resolved that only lines familiar from recitation should find recognition. Songs as such were out. But resolution faltered fairly soon. Gradually the plan disintegrated. Personal preference was pushed aside by other considerations. Regional balance, I felt, must be respected. I weighed the claims of Munster, Ulster, Leinster and Connacht. Even if numerical equity is achieved, can I stand over my distribution of gay and grave? Has Munster got all the patriotic fervour, Dublin all the laughs? Is the West awake? Then, of course, there is Orange and Green. Have I been fair to Cullybackey? Will Knocknagoshel rise in wrath? Have I given due representation to women? Granted that some of these pieces were written by women, would women recite them – or listen to them? Can any single mind encompass an appreciation of 'Tangmalangaloo' and 'A Pint of Plain is Your Only Man'? Is 'The Bells of Shandon' a eulogy, tongue-in-cheek doggerel, or downright mockery? And which or whether, what matter as long as I love it?

All this is not a plea for sympathy. Reservations and misgivings notwithstanding, I know that the vast wealth of material at our disposal ensures that any selection will be illustrative of 'Erin, the tear and the smile in thine eye'.

Finally we have the term 'Irish', which I have arbitrarily taken to mean 'of Irish origin' or concerned with Irish events or subject matter. However, there are people in Ireland, of all shades and shapes, who speak feelingly of Gunga Din and Dangerous Dan McGrew, the one-eyed yellow idol and the youth who bore 'mid snow and ice a banner with a strange device', to mention but a few. In salute to them I include 'Victoria-n-Edwardiana' by Vincent Caprani.

It was once customary to include in reciters a brief note of instruction on the art of delivery, with accompanying chart of 'useful and expressive gestures' and I have decided to revive this tradition. In these less formal times, however, my own recommendation would be a relaxed stance, glass in hand and this volume in the other.

Niall Toibin, 1986

ADVICE
on the Declamation
of Noble and Inspiring Verse
in Public Places
or for Private Satisfaction

YOU ARE URGED

1.   To impress hostile audiences that you are not alone by announcing boldly the author's name in full.

2.   To assume an aura of massive confidence. The opening lines should be enunciated unusually loudly with suitably striking gestures (see below), and light-minded persons fixed with a basilisk glare.

3.   To excite yourself with Missionary Zeal enough to combat that drably flat Worship of Obscurity preached by our morally depraved and musically debased university literature departments and examination-obsessed schoolteachers.

PRINCIPAL "POSITIONS" OF THE HANDS.

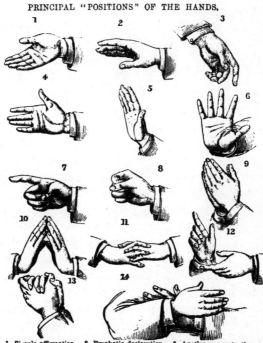

1. Simple affirmation.   2. Emphatic declaration.   3. Apathy or prostration.
4. Energetic appeal.   5. Negation or denial.   6. Violent repulsion.   7. Indexing or cautioning.   8. Determination or anger.   9. Supplication.   10. Gentle entreaty.
11. Carelessness.   12. Argumentativeness.   13. Earnest entreaty.   14. Resignation.

THE FOUR FARRELLYS

In a small hotel in London I was sitting down to dine,
When the waiter brought the register and asked me
   if I'd sign.
And as I signed I saw a name that set my heart
   astir –
A certain 'Francis Farrelly' had signed the register.
I knew a lot of Farrellys and out of all the crew
I kept on 'sort of wonderin' ' which Farrelly were
   you.
And when I'd finished dinner I sat back in my chair,
Going round my native land to find, what Farrelly
   you were.

SOUTH

Were you the keen-eyed Kerryman I met below
   Kenmare,
Who told me that when Ireland fought 'the odds
   were never fair'?
If Cromwell had met Sarsfield, or met Owen Roe
   O'Neill,
It's not to Misther Gladstone we'd be lookin' for
   repeal.
Would have Ireland for the Irish, not a Saxon to be
   seen,
And only Gaelic spoken in that House in College
   Green.
Told me landlords wor the Divil! their agints ten
   times worse,
And iv'ry sort of government for Ireland was a
   curse!
Oh! if you're that Francis Farrelly, your dreams have
   not come true,

1

Still, *Slainthe! Slainthe!* Fransheen! for I like a man
like you!

Or were you the Francis Farrelly that often used to
say
He'd like to blow them Papishes from Darry walls
away?
The boy who used to bother me that Orange Lodge
to join,
And thought that history started with the Battle o'
the Boyne –
I was not all with ye, Francis, the Pope is not ma
friend,
But still I hope, poor man, he'll die without that
bloody end –
And when yer quit from care yerself, and get to
Kingdom Come,
It's no use teachin' you the harp – you'll play the
Orange drum!
Och! man, ye wor a fighter, of that I had no doubt,
For I seen ye in Belfast one night when the Antrim
Road was out!
And many a time that evinin' I thought that ye wor
dead,
The way them Papish pavin' stones was hoppin' off
yer head.
Oh! if you're the Francis Farrelly who came from
north Tyrone –
Here's lookin' to ye, Francis, but do leave the Pope
alone!

EAST

Or were you the Francis Farrelly that in my college
days

2

For strolling on the Kingstown Pier had such a
   curious craze?
D'ye mind them lovely sisters – the blonde and the
   brunette?
I know I've not forgotten, and I don't think you
   forget!
That picnic at the Dargle – and the other at the
   Scalp –
How my heart was palpitatin' – hers wasn't – not a
   palp!
Someone said ye married money – and maybe ye were
   wise,
But the gold you loved was in her hair, and the
   di'monds in her eyes!
So I like to think ye married her and that you're with
   her yet,
'Twas some 'meleesha' officer that married the
   brunette;
But the blonde one always loved ye, and I knew you
   loved her too,
So me blessin's on ye, Francis, and the blue sky over
   you!

WEST

Or were you the Francis Farrelly I met so long
   ago,
In the bog below Belmullet, in the county of
   Mayo?
That long-legged, freckled Francis with the deep-set,
   wistful eyes,
That seemed to take their colour from those ever-
   changing skies.
That put his flute together as I sketched the distant
   scene,

And played me 'Planxty Kelly' and the 'Wakes of
   Inniskeen'.
That told me in the autumn he'd be sailin' to the
   west
To try and make his fortune and send money to the
   rest.
And would I draw a picture of the place where he
   was born,
And he'd hang it up, and look at it, and not feel so
   forlorn.
And when I had it finished, you got up from where
   you sat,
And you said, 'Well, you're the Divil, and I can't
   say more than that.'
Oh! if you're that Francis Farrelly, your fortune may
   be small,
But I'm thinking – thinking – Francis, that I love you
   best of all;
And I never can forget you – though it's years and
   years ago –
In the bog below Belmullet, in the county of Mayo.

Percy French
(1854–1920)

What shall we do for timber?
  The last of the woods is down,
Kilcash and the house of its glory
  And the bell of the house are gone;
.The spot where that lady waited
  Who shamed all women for grace,
When earls came sailing to greet her
  And Mass was said in the place.

My grief and my affliction
  Your gates are taken away,
Your avenue needs attention;
  Goats in the garden stray;
The courtyard's filled with water
  And the great earls where are they?
The earls, the lady, the people,
  Beaten into the clay.

No sound of duck or geese there,
  Hawk's cry or eagle's call,
No humming of the bees there
  That brought honey and wax for all,
Nor even the song of the birds there
  When the sun has gone down in the west,
Nor a cuckoo on top of the boughs there,
  Singing the world to rest.

There's mist there tumbling from branches
  Unstirred by night and by day,
And a darkness falling from heaven,
  And our fortunes have ebbed away;
There's no holly nor hazel nor ash there;
  The pasture is rock and stone,
The crown of the forest is withered
  And the last of its game is gone.

I beseech of Mary and Jesus
  That the great come home again,
With long dances danced in the garden,
  Fiddle music and mirth among men,
That Kilcash, the home of our fathers,
  Be lifted on high again,
And from that to the deluge of waters
  In bounty and peace remain.

Anonymous (18th century)
translated from the Irish by
Frank O'Connor
(1903–1966)

JOHN-JOHN

I dreamt last night of you, John-John,
   And thought you called to me;
And when I woke this morning, John,
   Yourself I hoped to see;
But I was all alone, John-John,
   Though still I heard your call:
I put my boots and bonnet on,
   And took my Sunday shawl,
And went, full sure to find you, John,
     To Nenagh fair.

The fair was just the same as then,
	Five years ago today,
When first you left the thimble men
	And came with me away;
For there again were thimble men
	And shooting galleries,
And card-trick men and Maggie men
	Of all sorts and degrees —
But not a sight of you, John-John,
		Was anywhere.

I turned my face to home again,
	And called myself a fool
To think you'd leave the thimble men
	And live again by rule,
And go to Mass and keep the fast
	And till the little patch:
My wish to have you home was past
	Before I raised the latch
And pushed the door and saw you, John,
		Sitting down there.

How cool you came in here, begad,
	As if you owned the place!
But rest yourself there now, my lad,
	'Tis good to see your face;
My dream is out, and now by it
	I think I know my mind:
At six o'clock this house you'll quit,
	And leave no grief behind; —
But until six o'clock, John-John,
		My bit you'll share.

My neighbours' shame of me began
   When first I brought you in;
To wed and keep a tinker man
   They thought a kind of sin;
But now this three year since you're gone
   'Tis pity me they do,
And that I'd rather have, John-John,
   Than that they'd pity you.
Pity for me and you, John-John,
        I could not bear.

Oh, you're my husband right enough,
   But what's the good of that?
You know you never were the stuff
   To be the cottage cat,
To watch the fire and hear me lock
   The door and put out Shep —
But there now, it is six o'clock
   And time for you to step.
God bless and keep you far, John-John!
        And that's my prayer.

Thomas MacDonagh
(1878–1916)

9

Seáġan · mac Caṫṁaoil · Del ·

THE MEMORY OF THE DEAD

Who fears to speak of Ninety-Eight?
 Who blushes at the name?
When cowards mock the patriot's fate,
 Who hangs his head for shame?
He's all a knave or half a slave
 Who slights his country thus:
But a true man, like you, man,
 Will fill your glass with us.

We drink the memory of the brave,
 The faithful and the few —
Some lie far off beyond the wave,
 Some sleep in Ireland, too;
All, all are gone — but still lives on
 The fame of those who died;
And true men, like you, men,
 Remember them with pride.

Some on the shores of distant lands
 Their weary hearts have laid,
And by the stranger's heedless hands
 Their lonely graves were made;
But though their clay be far away
 Beyond the Atlantic foam,
In true men, like you, men,
 Their spirit's still at home.

The dust of some is Irish earth;
    Among their own they rest;
And the same land that gave them birth
    Has caught them to her breast;
And we will pray that from their clay
    Full many a race may start
Of true men, like you, men,
    To act as brave a part.

They rose in dark and evil days
    To right their native land;
They kindled here a living blaze
    That nothing shall withstand.
Alas! that Might can vanquish Right –
    They fell, and passed away;
But true men, like you, men,
    Are plenty here today.

Then here's their memory – may it be
    For us a guiding light,
To cheer our strife for liberty,
    And teach us to unite!
Through good and ill, be Ireland's still,
    Though sad as theirs, your fate;
And true men, be you, men,
    Like those of Ninety-Eight.

John Kells Ingram
(1823–1907)

TORY PLEDGES

I pledge myself through thick and thin,
To labour still, with zeal devout,
To get the Outs, poor devils, in,
And turn the Ins, the wretches, out.

I pledge myself, though much bereft
Of ways and means of ruling ill,
To make the most of what are left,
And stick to all that's rotten still.

Though gone the days of place and pelf,
And drones no more take all the honey,
I pledge myself to cram myself
With all I can of public money;

To quarter on that social purse
My nephews, nieces, sisters, brothers,
Nor, so *we* prosper, care a curse
How much 'tis at the expense of others.

I pledge myself, whenever Right
And Might on any point divide,
Not to ask which is black or white,
But take, at once, the strongest side. . .

Betwixt the Corn-Lords and the Poor
I've not the slightest hesitation, –
The people *must* be starv'd to insure
The Land its due remuneration. . .

Such are the pledges I propose;
And though I can't now offer gold,
There's many a way of buying those
Who've but the taste for being sold.

So here's, with three times three hurrahs,
A toast, of which you'll not complain, –
'Long life to jobbing; may the days
Of Peculation shine again!'

Thomas Moore
(1779–1852)

It is suggested that the New Dances for the Winter Season should take their inspiration from the Politicians.

13

THE FAIRIES

Up the airy mountain,
    Down the rushy glen,
We daren't go a-hunting
    For fear of little men;
Wee folk, good folk,
    Trooping all together;
Green jacket, red cap,
    And white owl's feather!

Down along the rocky shore
    Some make their home –
They live on crispy pancakes
    Of yellow tide foam;
Some in the reeds
    Of the black mountain lake,
With frogs for their watchdogs,
    All night awake.

High on the hill-top
    The old King sits;
He is now so old and grey
    He's nigh lost his wits.
With a bridge of white mist,
    Columbkill he crosses,
On his stately journeys
    From Slieve League to Rosses;
Or going up with music
    On cold starry nights,
To sup with the Queen
    Of the gay Northern Lights.

14

They stole little Bridget
  For seven years long;
When she came down again
  Her friends were all gone.
They took her lightly back,
  Between the night and morrow;
They thought that she was fast asleep,
  But she was dead with sorrow.
They have kept her ever since
  Deep within the lakes,
On a bed of flag leaves,
  Watching till she wakes.

By the craggy hillside,
  Through the mosses bare,
They have planted thorn trees
  For pleasure here and there.
Is any man so daring
  As dig one up in spite,
He shall find their sharpest thorns
  In his bed at night.

Up the airy mountain,
  Down the rushy glen,
We daren't go a-hunting
  For fear of little men;
Wee folk, good folk,
  Trooping all together;
Green jacket, red cap,
  And white owl's feather!

William Allingham
(1824–1889)

15

THE COUNTY OF MAYO

On the deck of Patrick Lynch's boat I sat in
  woeful plight
Through my sighing all the weary day, and
  weeping all the night.
Were it not that full of sorrow from my people
  forth I go,
By the blessed sun! 'tis royally I'd sing thy
  praise, Mayo!

When I dwelt at home in plenty, and my gold did
  much abound,
In the company of fair young maids the Spanish
  ale went round.
'Tis a bitter change from those gay days that now
  I'm forced to go,
And must leave my bones in Santa Cruz, far from
  my own Mayo.

They are altered girls in Irrul now; 'tis proud
  they're grown and high,
With their hair-bags and their top-knots – for I
  pass their buckles by;
But it's little now I heed their airs, for God will
  have it so,
That I must depart for foreign lands, and leave my
  sweet Mayo.

'Tis my grief that Patrick Loughlin is not Earl of
    Irrul still,
And that Brian Duff no longer rules as Lord upon
    the hill,
And that Colonel Hugh MacGrady should be
    lying cold and low,
And I sailing, sailing swiftly from the county of
    Mayo.

Thomas Lavelle (17th century)
translated from the Irish by
George Fox
(1809–*c*. 1880)

THE LAKE ISLE OF INNISFREE

I will arise and go now, and go to Innisfree,
And a small cabin build there, of clay and wattles made,
Nine bean-rows will I have there, a hive for the honeybee,
And live alone in the bee-loud glade.

And I shall have some peace there, for peace comes
   dropping slow,
Dropping from the veils of the morning to where the
   cricket sings;
There midnight's all a glimmer, and noon a purple glow,
And evening full of the linnet's wings.

I will arise and go now, for always night and day
I hear lake water lapping with low sounds by the shore;
While I stand on the roadway, or on the pavements grey,
I hear it in the deep heart's core.

W.B. Yeats
(1865–1939)

18

GRACE FOR LIGHT

When we were little childer we had a quare wee house,
Away up in the heather by the head o' Brabla' burn;
The hares we'd see them scootin', an' we'd hear the
   crowin' grouse,
An' when we'd all be in at night ye'd not get room
   to turn.

The youngest two she'd put to bed, their faces to the wall,
An' the lave of us could sit aroun', just anywhere we might;
Herself 'ud take the rush-dip an' light it for us all,
An' 'God be thanked!' she would say, – 'now, we have
   a light.'

Then we be to quet the laughin' an' pushin' on the floor,
An' think on One who called us to come and be forgiven;
Himself 'ud put his pipe down, an' say the good word more,
'May the Lamb o' God lead us all to the Light o' Heaven!'

There's a wheen things that used to be an' now has had
   their day,
The nine glens of Antrim can show ye many a sight;
But not the quare wee house where we lived up Brabla' way,
Nor a child in all the nine glens that knows the grace
   for light.

Moira O'Neill
(1864–1955)

from THE DESERTED VILLAGE

Beside yon straggling fence that skirts the way,
With blossomed furze unprofitably gay,
There, in his noisy mansion, skilled to rule,
The village master taught his little school.
A man severe he was, and stern to view;
I knew him well, and every truant knew;
Well had the boding tremblers learned to trace
The day's disasters in his morning face;
Full well they laughed with counterfeited glee
At all his jokes, for many a joke had he;
Full well the busy whisper circling round
Conveyed the dismal tidings when he frowned.
Yet he was kind, or, if severe in aught,
The love he bore to learning was in fault;
The village all declared how much he knew:
'Twas certain he could write, and cipher too;
Lands he could measure, terms and tides presage,
And even the story ran that he could gauge;
In arguing, too, the parson owned his skill,
For, even though vanquished, he could argue still;
While words of learned length and thundering sound
Amazed the gazing rustics ranged around;
And still they gazed, and still the wonder grew,
That one small head could carry all he knew.

Oliver Goldsmith
(1728–1774)

21

WEE HUGHIE

He's gone to school, Wee Hughie,
An' him not four,
Sure I saw the fright was in him
When he left the door.

But he took a hand o' Denny
An' a hand o' Dan,
Wi' Joe's owld coat upon him —
Och, the poor wee man!

He cut the quarest figure,
More stout nor thin;
An' trottin' right an' steady
Wi' his toes turned in.

I watched him to the corner
O' the big turf stack,
An' the more his feet went forrit,
Still his head turned back.

He was lookin', would I call him —
Och, me heart was woe —
Sure it's lost I am without him,
But he be to go.

I followed to the turnin'
When they passed it by,
God help him, he was cryin',
An', maybe, so was I.

Elizabeth Shane
(?–1951)

WHEN I WAS TWENTY-WAN

It's a stormy night, my pipe's alight, and I sit me
    by the fire,
With a divil a soul to disturb me, save the cat,
    and the kittens by her,
I'll hitch my chair – a black oak log – right up
    again' the brace,
And cross me legs in comfort, and smoke me
    pipe in paice;
I'd like to have a *seanach*, now, with Rory or
    with Dan,
Or any of the boys I knew when I was
    Twenty-wan.

But, no: for Rory's gone long since, and Dan is
 gone likewise,
And many another – like that puff, they started
 for the skies!
Ye're most an' ould man now yourself – come
 Lammas, seventy-seven –
And ould Time is thrinnlin' ye fast, me lad, to the
 goolden gates of heaven;
Faith Mick, me boy, it's quare to think what
 droll things filled your span –
There's changes, troth, and strange ones, since
 you were Twenty-wan!

Ye mind the day that Una tripped with you unto
 the altar,
And Father Peter laid on yous the matrimonial
 halter?
Ye mind her sweet wee face, *a gradh,* dark hair,
 and sloe-black eyes,
That murdered many a stout lad's heart ere you
 bore off the prize?
Ye carried a head as high them times as any in the
 lan', –
For throgs ye were consaited, when ye were
 Twenty-wan.

And maybe with some raison, too, for ye were
 strong and hale,
And tall, and straight as a rowan tree, with heart
 that couldn't quail;
Ye were first at heavin' the shoulder-stone, and
 first at *camán* play;
And your features was well-favoured, too, the
 neighbours used to say,
But howsomever that may be, at laist it's true,
 me man,
The girls admired Mick Moran when he was
 Twenty-wan.

And, och! how Irish girls have changed in the
    years that's gone since then,
They aren't sure the same *cailíns* they used to be,
    me frien';
But takin' afther foreign dames, and dressin' up
    like dolls,
With under-skirts, and over-skirts, and frills,
    and foldherols,
With fringes, flounces, *fishies*, and kid gloves,
    and a fan –
The sorra dhraim such sins, they did, when I was
    Twenty-wan.

No; Una looked far prettier in striped petticoat,
    I vow;
She cut no haythin monkey-fringe to hide her
    sweet, white brow,
The tightest stay she ever wore was my arm
    aroun' her waist,
And when your lips met hers, *a mhic*, it wasn't
    paint ye'd taste:
She wore no basket-bonnet, and no hat like a
    pan,
And the sorra take the *fishy* when I was Twenty-
    wan!

They're talkin' still of Irelan' – her rights and
    wrongs and woes;
And for redress they're callin' – prayin' to her
    foes;
It seems to me – though I am ould, and maybe in
    the wrong –
The logic long ago we used was readier, and
    more sthrong, –
In my young days, each took a pike and rose up
    to a man;
'Wrong, wrong!' ye say – well, blood was hot
    when I was Twenty-wan.

The worl' has grown mortial wise, and wisdom's
    still the rage,
Troth, Mick, me frien', I sorely doubt your far
    behin' your age;
Your musty ould-worl' notions, sure, of what is
    wrong and right
The lads that's primed with larnin' now, would
    call plain blatherskite –
But still, I say, if larnin' goes with cunnin' han' in
    han',
Give me the honest ignorance I foun' at Twenty-
    wan!

Well, God be thankit! ye had cares and troubles
    in your day,
But bore them, knowin' thoroughly the Man-
    Above's good pay;
And ye weren't throgs mistaken – for, now ye're
    ould and ripe,
Sure your days glide like the smoke-wreaths
    there, that's curlin' from your pipe;
And lake that pipe you'll soon go out, – to ashes
    turn, me man –
Just as ye've seen your comrades go since
    glorious Twenty-wan!

Seumas MacManus
(*c.* 1868–1960)

AN OLD WOMAN OF THE ROADS

Oh, to have a little house!
  To own the hearth and stool and all!
The heaped-up sods upon the fire,
  The pile of turf against the wall!

To have a clock with weights and chains
  And pendulum swinging up and down!
A dresser filled with shining delph,
  Speckled and white and blue and brown!

I could be busy all the day
  Clearing and sweeping hearth and floor,
And fixing on their shelf again
  My white and blue and speckled store!

I could be quiet there at night
  Beside the fire and by myself,
Sure of a bed, and loth to leave
  The ticking clock and the shining delph!

Och! but I'm weary of mist and dark,
  And roads where there's never a house or bush,
And tired I am of bog and road
  And the crying wind and the lonesome hush!

And I am praying to God on high,
  And I am praying Him night and day,
For a little house – a house of my own –
  Out of the wind's and the rain's way.

Padraic Colum
(1881–1972)

28

THE BELLS OF SHANDON

'Sabbata pango,
Funera plango,
Solemnia clango'
Inscription on an old bell

With deep affection
And recollection
I often think of
   Those Shandon bells,
Whose sounds so wild would
In the days of childhood
Fling round my cradle
   Their magic spells.
On this I ponder
Where'er I wander,
And thus grow fonder
   Sweet Cork, of thee;
With thy bells of Shandon,
That sound so grand on
The pleasant waters
   Of the river Lee.

I've heard bells chiming
Full many a clime in,
Tolling sublime in
   Cathedral shrine,
While at a glib rate
Brass tongues would vibrate –
But all their music
   Spoke naught like thine;
For memory dwelling
On each proud swelling
Of the belfry knelling
   Its bold notes free,
Made the bells of Shandon
Sound far more grand on
The pleasant waters
   Of the river Lee.

I've heard bells tolling
Old 'Adrian's Mole' in,
Their thunder rolling
   From the Vatican,
And cymbals glorious
Swinging uproarious
In the gorgeous turrets
   Of Notre Dame;
But thy sounds were sweeter
Than the dome of Peter
Flings o'er the Tiber,
   Pealing solemnly; –
O! the bells of Shandon
Sound far more grand on
The pleasant waters
   Of the river Lee.

There's a bell in Moscow,
While on tower and kiosk, O!
In Saint Sophia
    The Turkman gets,
And loud in air
Calls men to prayer
From the tapering summit
    Of tall minarets.
Such empty phantom
I freely grant them;
But there is an anthem
    More dear to me, –
'Tis the bells of Shandon
That sound so grand on
The pleasant waters
    Of the river Lee.

Francis Sylvester Mahony (Father Prout)
(1804–1866)

CAOCH O'LEARY

One winter's day, long, long ago,
  When I was a little fellow,
A piper wandered to our door,
  Grey-headed, blind, and yellow –
And, oh! how glad was my young heart,
  Though earth and sky looked dreary –
To see the stranger and his dog –
  Poor 'Pinch' and Caoch O'Leary.

And when he stowed away his 'bag',
  Cross-barred with green and yellow,
I thought and said, 'in Ireland's ground,
  There's not so fine a fellow',
And Finian Burke and Seán Magee,
  And Eily, Kate, and Mary,
Rushed in with panting haste to 'see',
  And 'welcome' Caoch O'Leary.

Oh! God be with those happy times,
  Oh! God be with my childhood,
When I, bare-headed, roamed all day
  Bird-nesting in the wild-wood –
I'll not forget those sunny hours,
  However years may vary,
I'll not forget my early friends,
  Nor honest Caoch O'Leary.

Poor Caoch and 'Pinch' slept well that night,
    And in the morning early,
He called me up to hear him play
    'The wind that shakes the barley';
And then he stroked my flaxen hair,
    And cried – 'God mark my "deary"',
And how I wept when he said, 'Farewell,
    And think of Caoch O'Leary.'

And seasons came and went, and still
    Old Caoch was not forgotten,
Although I thought him 'dead and gone',
    And in the cold clay rotten.
And often when I walked and danced
    With Eily, Kate, and Mary,
We spoke of childhood's rosy hours,
    And prayed for Caoch O'Leary.

Well – twenty summers had gone past,
    And June's red sun was sinking,
When I, a man, sat by my door,
    Of twenty sad things thinking.
A little dog came up the way,
    His gait was slow and weary,
And at his tail a lame man limped –
    'Twas 'Pinch' and Caoch O'Leary!

Old Caoch! but ah! how woe-begone!
    His form is bowed and bending,
His fleshless hands are stiff and wan,
    Ay – time is even blending
The colours on his threadbare 'bag' –
    And 'Pinch' is twice as hairy
And 'thinspare' as when first I saw
    Himself and Caoch O'Leary.

'God's blessing here!' the wanderer cried,
    'Far, far, be hell's black viper;
Does anybody hereabouts
    Remember Caoch the Piper?'
With swelling heart I grasped his hand;
    The old man murmured 'Deary!
Are you the silky-headed child
    That loved poor Caoch O'Leary?'

'Yes, yes,' I said – the wanderer wept
    As if his heart was breaking –
'And where, *a mhic mo chroidhe,*' he sobbed,
    'Is all the merry-making
I found here twenty years ago?'
    'My tale,' I sighed, 'might weary,
Enough to say – there's none but me
    To welcome Caoch O'Leary.'

'Vo, Vo, Vo, Vo!' the old man cried,
    And wrung his hands in sorrow,
'Pray lead me in, *a stór mo chroidhe,*
    And I'll go home tomorrow.
My peace is made – I'll calmly leave
    This world so cold and dreary,
And you shall keep my pipes and dog,
    And pray for Caoch O'Leary.'

With 'Pinch' I watched his bed that night,
    Next day, his wish was granted;
He died – and Father James was brought,
    And Requiem Mass was chanted –
The neighbours came – we dug his grave,
    Near Eily, Kate, and Mary;
And there he sleeps his last sweet sleep –
    God rest you! Caoch O'Leary.

John Keegan
(1809–1849)

35

THE FIGHTING RACE

'Read out the names!' and Burke sat back,
    And Kelly drooped his head,
While Shea – they call him Scholar Jack –
    Went down the list of the dead.
Officers, seamen, gunners, marines,
    The crews of the gig and yawl,
The bearded man and the lad in his teens,
    Carpenters, coal passers – all.
Then, knocking the ashes from out his pipe,
    Said Burke in an offhand way:
'We're all in that dead man's list, by Cripe!
    Kelly and Burke and Shea.'
'Well, here's to the Maine, and I'm sorry for Spain,'
    Said Kelly and Burke and Shea.

'Wherever there's Kellys there's trouble,' said Burke.
    'Wherever fighting's the game,
Or a spice of danger in grown man's work,'
    Said Kelly, 'you'll find my name.'
'And do we fall short,' said Burke, getting mad,
    'When it's touch-and-go for life?'
Said Shea, 'It's thirty-odd years, bedad,
    Since I charged to drum and fife
Up Marye's Heights, and my old canteen
    Stopped a rebel ball on its way.
There were blossoms of blood on our sprigs of green –
    Kelly and Burke and Shea –
And the dead didn't brag.' 'Well, here's to the flag!'
    Said Kelly and Burke and Shea.

36

'I wish't was in Ireland, for there's the place,'
  Said Burke, 'that we'd die by right,
In the cradle of our soldier race,
  After one good stand-up fight.
My grandfather fell on Vinegar Hill,
  And fighting was not his trade;
But his rusty pike's in the cabin still,
  With Hessian blood on the blade.'
'Aye, aye,' said Kelly, 'the pikes were great
  When the word was "clear the way!"
We were thick on the roll in Ninety-Eight —
  Kelly and Burke and Shea.'
'Well, here's to the pike and the sword and the like!'
  Said Kelly and Burke and Shea.

And Shea, the scholar, with rising joy,
  Said, 'We were at Ramillies;
We left our bones at Fontenoy
  And up in the Pyrenees.
Before Dunkirk, on Landen's plain,
  Cremona, Lille, and Ghent,
We're all over Austria, France, and Spain,
  Wherever they pitched a tent.
We've died for England from Waterloo
  To Egypt and Dargai;
And still there's enough for a corps or a crew,
  Kelly and Burke and Shea.'
'Well, here is to good honest fighting blood!'
  Said Kelly and Burke and Shea.

'Oh, the fighting races don't die out,
  If they seldom die in bed,
For love is first in their hearts, no doubt,'
  Said Burke; then Kelly said:
'When Michael, the Irish archangel, stands,
  The angel with the sword,
And the battle-dead from a hundred lands
  Are ranged in one big horde,
Our line, that for Gabriel's trumpet waits,
  Will stretch three deep that day,
From Jehoshaphat to the Golden Gates –
  Kelly and Burke and Shea.'
'Well, here's thank God for the race and the sod!'
  Said Kelly and Burke and Shea.

Joseph I.C. Clarke
(1846–1925)

38

THE BALLAD OF THE TINKER'S DAUGHTER

When rooks ripped home at eventide
And trees pegged shadows to the ground,
The tinkers came to Carhan bridge
And camped beside the Famine mound,

With long-eared ass and bony horse,
And blue-wheeled cart and caravan,
And she, the fairest of them all,
The daughter of the tinker clan.

The sun flamed in her red, red hair
And in her eyes danced stars of mirth,
Her body held the willow's grace,
Her feet scarce touched the springing earth.

The night spread its star-tasselled shawls,
The river gossiped to its stones,
She sat beside the leaping fire
And sang the songs the tinker owns:

The songs as old as turning wheels
And sweet as bird-throats after rain,
Deep wisdom of the wild wet earth,
The pain of joy, the joy of pain.

A farmer going by the road
To tend his cattle in the byre
And saw her like some fairy queen
Between the river and the fire.

Her beauty stirred his brooding blood,
Her magic mounted in his head,
He stole her from her tinker clan
And on the morrow they were wed.

And when the sunlight swamped the hills
And bird-song drowned the river's bells,
The tinkers quenched their hazel fires
And climbed the windy road to Kells.

And from this house she watched them go
With blue-wheeled cart and caravan,
The long-eared ass and bony horse,
And brown-haired woman and tinker man.

She watched them go, she watched them fade
And vanish in the yellow furze;
A cold wind blew across the sun
And silenced all the singing birds.

She saw the months run on and on,
And heard the river fret and foam,
At white of day the roosters called,
At dim of dusk the cows came home.

The crickets strummed their heated harps
In hidden halls behind the hob,
And told of distant waterways
Where the black moorhens dive and bob,

And shoot the glassy bubbles up
To smash their windows on the stones;
And brown trout hide their spots of gold
Among the river's pebbly bones;

And, too, the ebbing sea that flung
A net of sound about the stars,
Set strange hills dancing in her dreams
And meshed her to the wandering cars.

She stole out from her sleeping man
And fled the fields that tied her down,
Her face moved towards the rising sun,
Her back was to the tired town.

She climbed the pallid road to Kells,
Against the hill, against the wind,
In Glenbeigh of the mountain-streams,
She came among her tinker-kind.

They bedded her between the wheels
And there her son was born,
She heard the tinker-woman's praise
Before she died that morn. . .

The years flew by like frightened birds
That spill a feather and are gone,
The farmer walked his weedful fields
And made the tinkers travel on.

No more they camped by Carhan bridge
And coaxed their fires to fragrant flame,
They saw him with his dog and gun,
They spat and cursed his name.

And when May hid the hawthorn trees
With stars she stole from out the skies,
There came a barefoot tinker lad
With red, red hair and laughing eyes.

He left the road, he crossed the fields,
The farmer shot him in the side,
The smile went from his twisting lips,
He told his name and died.

That evening when the neighbours came
They found the son laid on the floor,
And saw the father swinging dead
Between the window and the door.

They placed the boy upon the cart
And cut the swaying farmer down,
They swear a tinker woman came
With them all the way to town.

The sun flamed in her red, red hair,
And in her eyes danced stars of mirth,
Her body held the willow's grace,
Her feet scarce touched the springing earth.

They buried them in Keelvarnogue
And eyes were moist and lips were wan,
And when the mound was patted down
The tinker maid was gone.

These things were long before my day,
I only speak with borrowed words,
But that is how the story goes
In Iveragh of the singing birds.

Sigerson Clifford
(1913–1985)

42

I SHALL NOT DIE

I shall not die because of you
   O woman though you shame the swan,
They were foolish men you killed,
   Do not think me a foolish man.

Why should I leave the world behind
   For the soft hand, the dreaming eye,
The crimson lips, the breasts of snow –
   Is it for these you'd have me die?

Why should I heed the fancy free,
   The joyous air, the eye of blue,
The side like foam, the virgin neck?
   I shall not die because of you.

The devil take the golden hair!
   That maiden look, that voice so gay,
That delicate heel and pillared thigh
   Only some foolish man would slay.

O woman though you shame the swan
   A wise man taught me all he knew,
I know the crooked ways of love,
   I shall not die because of you.

Anonymous (16th century)
translated from the Irish by
Frank O'Connor
(1903–1966)

ACH, I DUNNO!

I'm simply surrounded by lovers
   Since Da made his fortune in land.
They're comin' in crowds like the plovers
   To ax for me hand –
There's clerks and policemen and teachers,
   Some sandy, some black as a crow –
Ma says you get used to the creatures
       But, ach, I dunno!

The convent is in a commotion
   To think of me taking a spouse,
And they wonder I hadn't the notion
   Of taking the vows.
'Tis a beautiful life and a quiet,
   And keeps ye from going below,
As a girl I thought I might try it,
       But, ach, I dunno!

I've none but meself to look after,
   An' marriage it fills me with fears,
I think I'd have less of the laughter
   And more of the tears.
I'll not be a slave like me mother,
   With six of us all in a row,
Even one little baby's a bother,
       But, ach, I dunno!

There's a lad that has taken me fancy,
  I know he's a bit of a limb,
And though marriage is terrible chancy,
  I'd – chance it with him.
He's coming tonight – oh – I tingle,
  From the top of me head to me toe,
I'll tell him I'd rather live single,
    But, ach, I dunno!

Percy French
(1854–1920)

45

THE SONG OF WANDERING AENGUS

I went out to the hazel wood,
Because a fire was in my head,
And cut and peeled a hazel wand,
And hooked a berry to a thread;
And when white moths were on the wing,
And moth-like stars were flickering out,
I dropped the berry in a stream
And caught a little silver trout.

When I had laid it on the floor
I went to blow the fire aflame,
But something rustled on the floor,
And some one called me by my name:
It had become a glimmering girl
With apple blossom in her hair
Who called me by my name and ran
And faded through the brightening air.

Though I am old with wandering
Through hollow lands and hilly lands,
I will find out where she has gone,
And kiss her lips and take her hands;
And walk among long dappled grass,
And pluck till time and times are done
The silver apples of the moon,
The golden apples of the sun.

W.B. Yeats
(1865–1939)

46

from THE MIDNIGHT COURT

My chief complaint and principal grief,
The thing that gives me no relief,
Sweeps me from harbour in my mind
And blows me like smoke on every wind
Is all the girls whose charms miscarry
Throughout the land and who'll never marry;
Bitter old maids without house or home,
Put on one side through no fault of their own.
I know myself from the things I've seen
Enough and to spare of the sort I mean,
And to give an example, here am I
While the tide is flowing, left high and dry.
Wouldn't you think I must be a fright,
To be shelved before I get started right;
Heartsick, bitter, dour and wan,
Unable to sleep for the want of a man?
But how can I lie in a lukewarm bed
With all the thoughts that come into my head?
Indeed, 'tis time that somebody stated
The way that the women are situated,
For if men go on their path to destruction
There will nothing be left to us but abduction.
Their appetite wakes with age and blindness
When you'd let them cover you only from kindness,
And offer it up for the wrongs you'd done
In hopes of reward in the life to come:
And if one of them weds in the heat of youth
When the first down is on his mouth
It isn't some woman of his own sort,
Well-shaped, well-mannered or well-taught;
Some mettlesome girl who studied behaviour,
To sit and stand and amuse a neighbour,
But some pious old prude or dour defamer
Who sweated the couple of pounds that shame her.

47

48

There you have it! It has me melted,
And makes me feel that the world's demented:
A county's choice for brains and muscle,
Fond of a lark and not scared of a tussle,
Decent and merry and sober and steady,
Good-looking, gamesome, rakish and ready;
A boy in the blush of his youthful vigour
With a gracious flush and a passable figure
Finds a fortune the best attraction
And sires himself off on some bitter extraction;
Some fretful old maid with her heels in the dung,
Pious airs and venomous tongue,
Vicious and envious, nagging and whining,
Snoozing and snivelling, plotting, contriving —
Hell to her soul, an unmannerly sow
With a pair of bow legs and hair like tow
Went off this morning to the altar
And here am I still without hope of the halter!
Couldn't some man love me as well?
Amn't I plump and sound as a bell?
Lips for kissing and teeth for smiling,
Blossomy skin and forehead shining?
My eyes are blue and my hair is thick
And coils in streams about my neck —
A man who's looking for a wife,
Here's a face that will keep for life!
Hand and arm and neck and breast,
Each is better than the rest.
Look at that waist! My legs are long,
Limber as willows and light and strong.
There's bottom and belly that claim attention,
And the best concealed that I needn't mention.

Bryan Merryman (18th century)
translated from the Irish by
Frank O'Connor
(1903–1966)

49

SONG FOR THE CLATTER-BONES

God rest that Jewy woman,
Queen Jezebel, the bitch
Who peeled the clothes from her shoulder-bones
Down to her spent teats
As she stretched out of the window
Among the geraniums, where
She chaffed and laughed like one half daft
Titivating her painted hair –

King Jehu he drove to her
She tipped him a fancy beck;
But he from his knacky side-car spoke,
'Who'll break that dewlapped neck?'
And so she was thrown from the window,
Like Lucifer she fell
Beneath the feet of the horses and they beat
The light out of Jezebel.

That corpse wasn't planted in clover,
Ah, nothing of her was found
Save those grey bones that Hare-foot Mike
Gave me for their lovely sound;
And as once her dancing body
Made star-lit princes sweat,
So I'll just clack: though her ghost lacks a back
There's music in the old bones yet.

F.R. Higgins
(1896–1941)

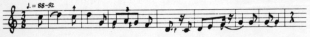

50

ME AN' ME DA

I'm livin' in Drumlister,
   An' I'm gettin' very oul',
I have to wear an Indian bag
   To save me from the coul'.
The deil a man in this townlan'
   Wos claner raired nor me,
But I'm livin' in Drumlister
   In clabber to the knee.

Me da lived up in Carmin,
   An' kep' a sarvint boy;
His second wife wos very sharp,
   He birried her with joy:
Now she wos thin, her name was Flynn,
   She comes from Cullentra,
An' if me shirt's a clatty shirt
   The man to blame's me da.

Consarnin' weemin, sure it wos
   A constant word of his,
'Keep far away from them that's thin,
   Their temper's aisy riz.'
Well, I knowed two I thought wud do,
   But still I had me fears,
So I kiffled back an' forrit
   Between the two, for years.

Wee Margit had no fortune
　　But two rosy cheeks wud plaze;
The farm of lan' wos Bridget's,
　　But she tuk the pock disayse:
An' Margit she wos very wee,
　　An' Bridget she wos stout,
But her face wos like a gaol dure
　　With the bowlts pulled out.

I'll tell no lie on Margit,
　　She thought the worl' of me;
I'll tell the thruth, me heart wud lep
　　The sight of her to see.
But I wos slow, ye surely know,
　　The raison of it now,
If I left her home from Carmin
　　Me da wud rise a row.

So I swithered back an' forrit
　　Till Margit got a man;
A fella come from Mullaslin
　　An' left me jist the wan.
I mind the day she went away,
　　I hid wan strucken hour,
An' cursed the wasp from Cullentra
　　That made me da so sour.

But cryin' cures no trouble,
　　To Bridget I went back,
An' faced her for it that night week
　　Beside her own thurf-stack.
I axed her there, an' spoke her fair,
　　The handy wife she'd make me,
I talked about the lan' that joined
　　– Begob, she wudn't take me!

So I'm livin' in Drumlister,
    An' I'm gettin' very oul'
I creep to Carmin wanst a month
    To thry an' make me sowl:
The deil a man in this townlan'
    Wos claner raired nor me,
An' I'm dyin' in Drumlister
    In clabber to the knee.

W.F. Marshall
(1888–1959)

DARK ROSALEEN

O, my Dark Rosaleen,
  Do not sigh, do not weep!
The priests are on the ocean green,
  They march along the deep.
There's wine from the royal Pope,
  Upon the ocean green;
And Spanish ale shall give you hope,
  My Dark Rosaleen!
  My own Rosaleen!
Shall glad your heart, shall give you hope,
Shall give you health, and help, and hope.
  My Dark Rosaleen!

Over hills, and thro' dales,
  Have I roam'd for your sake;
All yesterday I sail'd with sails
  On river and on lake.
The Erne, at its highest flood,
  I dash'd across unseen,
For there was lightning in my blood,
  My Dark Rosaleen!
  My own Rosaleen!
O, there was lightning in my blood,
Red lightning lighten'd thro' my blood.
  My Dark Rosaleen!

All day long, in unrest,
    To and fro, do I move.
The very soul within my breast
    Is wasted for you, love!
The heart in my bosom faints
    To think of you, my Queen,
My life of life, my saint of saints,
    My Dark Rosaleen!
    My own Rosaleen!
To hear your sweet and sad complaints,
My life, my love, my saint of saints,
    My Dark Rosaleen!

Woe and pain, pain and woe,
    Are my lot, night and noon,
To see your bright face clouded so,
    Like to the mournful moon.
But yet will I rear your throne
    Again in golden sheen;
'Tis you shall reign, shall reign alone,
    My Dark Rosaleen!
    My own Rosaleen!
'Tis you shall have the golden throne,
'Tis you shall reign, and reign alone,
    My Dark Rosaleen!

Over dews, over sands,
    Will I fly, for your weal:
Your holy delicate white hands
    Shall girdle me with steel.
At home, in your emerald bowers,
    From morning's dawn till e'en,
You'll pray for me, my flower of flowers,
    My Dark Rosaleen!
    My fond Rosaleen!
You'll think of me through daylight hours,
My virgin flower, my flower of flowers,
    My Dark Rosaleen!

56

I could scale the blue air,
   I could plough the high hills,
Oh, I could kneel all night in prayer,
   To heal your many ills!
And one beamy smile from you
   Would float like light between
My toils and me, my own, my true,
   My Dark Rosaleen!
   My fond Rosaleen!
Would give me life and soul anew,
A second life, a soul anew,
   My Dark Rosaleen!

O, the Erne shall run red,
   With redundance of blood,
The earth shall rock beneath our tread
   And flames wrap hill and wood,
And gun-peal and slogan-cry
   Wake many a glen serene,
Ere you shall fade, ere you shall die,
   My Dark Rosaleen!
   My own Rosaleen!
The Judgement Hour must first be nigh,
Ere you can fade, ere you can die,
   My Dark Rosaleen!

Anonymous (16th century)
translated from the Irish by
J.C. Mangan
(1803–1849)

A PINT OF PLAIN IS YOUR ONLY MAN

When things go wrong and will not come right,
Though you do the best you can,
When life looks black as the hour of night —
A pint of plain is your only man.

When money's tight and is hard to get
And your horse has also ran,
When all you have is a heap of debt —
A pint of plain is your only man.

When health is bad and your heart feels strange,
And your face is pale and wan,
When doctors say that you need a change —
A pint of plain is your only man.

When food is scarce and your larder bare
And no rashers grease your pan,
When hunger grows as your meals are rare —
A pint of plain is your only man.

In time of trouble and lousy strife,
You have still got a darlint plan,
You still can turn to a brighter life —
A pint of plain is your only man.

Flann O'Brien
(1911–1966)

from DRUNKEN THADY AND THE BISHOP'S LADY

. . .There lived and died in Limerick city
A dame of fame – oh! what a pity
That dames of fame should live and die,
And never learn for what or why!
Some say her maiden name was Brady
And others say she was a Grady. . .
'Tis true she lived, 'tis true she died,
'Tis true she was a bishop's bride,

But for herself 'twas little matter
To whom she had been wife or daughter. . .
Spending the Reverend Lordship's treasure,
Chasing the world's evil pleasure.
In love with suppers, cars and balls,
And luxurious sin of festive halls
Where flaming hearts and flaming wine
Invite the passions all to dine.

She died – her actions were recorded –
Whether in heaven or hell rewarded
We know not; but her time was given
Without a thought of hell or heaven.
Her days and nights were spent in mirth,
She made a genial heaven of earth,
And never dreamt, at balls or dinners,
There is a hell to punish sinners. . .

Death steals behind the smile of joy
With weapons ready to destroy. . .
And when the fated hour is ready
He cares not for a lord or lady,
But lifts his gun and snaps the trigger
And shoots alike the king and beggar.
And thus the heroine of our tale
He shot, as fowlers shoot a quail. . .

But now I have some secret notion
She did not like her new promotion,
For if she did, she would remain,
And scorn to come to earth again.
But earth, the home of her affection,
Could not depart her recollection,
So, she returned to flash and shine,
But never more to dance or dine. . .

Each night she roamed with airy feet
From Thomond Bridge to Castle Street,
And those that stayed out past eleven
Would want a special guard from heaven
To shield them with a holy wand
From the mad terrors of her hand. . .

No pugilist in Limerick town
Could knock a man so quickly down
Or deal an active blow so ready
To floor one, as the Bishop's Lady.
And, thus, the ghost appear'd and vanish'd
Until her Ladyship was banish'd
By Father Power, whom things of evil
Dreaded, as mortals dread the devil. . .

But ere the Priest removed the Lady,
There lived a chap called Drunken Thady
In Thomondgate, of social joys,
The birthplace of the devil's boys.
Thade knew his country's history well
And for her sake would go to hell. . .
In heart he was an Irish Lumper,
But all his glory was a bumper.

He believed in God right firm and well,
But served no heaven and feared no hell.
A sermon on hell's pains may start him,

It may convince, but not convert him.
He knew his failing and his fault
Lay in the tempting drop of malt;
And every day his vice went further,
And as he drank, his heart grew harder. . .

But Thady loved intoxication
And foil'd all hopes of reformation,
He still raised rows and drank the whiskey
And roar'd just like the Bay of Biscay. . .
The jail received him forty times
For midnight rows and drunken crimes.
He flailed his wife and thumped his brother
And burn'd the bed about his mother. . .

All day he drank poteen at Hayes's
And pitched the King and Law to blazes. . .
'Twas Christmas Eve – the gale was high –
The snow-clouds swept along the sky. . .
But Thady felt no hail, nor sleet,
As home he reel'd thro' Castle Street. . .
And, giddy as a summer midge,
Went staggering towards old Thomond Bridge
Whose fourteen arches braved so clever
Six hundred years the rapid river. . .

His thoughts were on the Bishop's Lady –
The first tall arch was crossed already –
He paused upon the haunted ground,
The barrier of her midnight round.
Along the bridge-way, dark and narrow,
He peep'd – while terror drove its arrow,
Cold as the keen blast of October,
Thro' all his frame and made him sober.

Awhile he stood, in doubt suspended,
Still to push forward he intended,

When, lo! just as his fears released him,
Up came the angry ghost and seized him. . .
He saw her face, grim, large and pale,
Her red eyes sparkled thro' her veil,
Her scarlet cloak — half immaterial —
Flew wildly round her person aerial.

With oaths he tried to grasp her form —
'Twas easier far to catch a storm.
Before his eyes she held him there,
His hands felt nothing more than air;
Her grasp press'd on him cold as steel,
He saw the form, but could not feel.
He tried not, tho' his brain was dizzy,
To kiss *her*, as he kissed Miss Lizzy,
But prayed to heaven for help sincere —
The first time e'er he said a prayer.

'Twas vain! the spirit in her fury,
To do her work was in a hurry;
And rising with a whirlwind's strength,
Hurl'd him o'er the battlement.
Splash! went poor Thady in the torrent
And roll'd along the rapid current,
Towards Curragour's mad-roaring fall
The billows tossed him like a ball.
And who dare say, that saw him sinking,
But 'twas his last full round of drinking?

Yet, no! against the river's might
He made a long and gallant fight;
That stream in which he learned to swim
Shall be no watery grave to him. . .
Above the fall, he spied afloat
Some object like an anchor'd boat.
To this with furious grasp he clung,
And from the tide his limbs upswung.

Half-frozen in the stern he lay
Until the holy light of day
Brought forth some kind assisting hand
To row poor Thady to the strand.
'Mid gazing crowds he left the shore,
Well sobered, and got drunk no more!
And in the whole wide parish round
A better Christian was not found:
He loved his God, and served his neighbour,
And earn'd his bread by honest labour.

Michael Hogan,
the Bard of Thomond (1832–1899)
abridged by
Niall Toibin
(1929–   )

RINGSEND

After reading Tolstoi

I will live in Ringsend
With a red-headed whore,
And the fan-light gone in
Where it lights the hall-door;
And listen each night
For her querulous shout,
As at last she streels in
And the pubs empty out.
To soothe that wild breast
With my old-fangled songs,
Till she feels it redressed
From inordinate wrongs,
Imagined, outrageous,
Preposterous wrongs,
Till peace at last comes,
Shall be all I will do,
Where the little lamp blooms
Like a rose in the stew;
And up the back-garden
The sound comes to me
Of the lapsing, unsoilable,
Whispering sea.

Oliver St John Gogarty
(1878–1957)

A GLASS OF BEER

The lanky hank of a she in the inn over there
Nearly killed me for asking the loan of a glass of beer;
May the devil grip the whey-faced slut by the hair,
And beat bad manners out of her skin for a year.

That parboiled ape, with the toughest jaw you will see
On virtue's path, and a voice that would rasp the dead,
Came roaring and raging the minute she looked at me,
And threw me out of the house on the back of my head!

If I asked her master he'd give me a cask a day;
But she, with the beer at hand, not a gill would arrange!
May she marry a ghost and bear him a kitten, and may
The High King of Glory permit her to get the mange.

James Stephens
(*c.* 1882–1950)

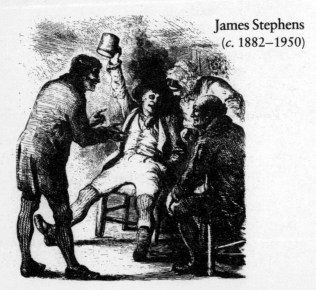

66

IF EVER YOU GO TO DUBLIN TOWN

If ever you go to Dublin town
In a hundred years or so
Inquire for me in Baggot Street
And what I was like to know.
O he was a queer one,
Fol dol the di do,
He was a queer one
I tell you.

My great-grandmother knew him well,
He asked her to come and call
On him in his flat and she giggled at the thought
Of a young girl's lovely fall.
O he was dangerous,
Fol dol the di do,
He was dangerous
I tell you.

On Pembroke Road look out for my ghost,
Dishevelled with shoes untied,
Playing through the railings with little children
Whose children have long since died.
O he was a nice man,
Fol dol the di do,
He was a nice man
I tell you.

Go into a pub and listen well
If my voice still echoes there,
Ask the men what their grandsires thought
And tell them to answer fair.
O he was eccentric,
Fol dol the di do,
He was eccentric
I tell you.

He had the knack of making men feel
As small as they really were
Which meant as great as God had made them
But as males they disliked his air.
O he was a proud one,
Fol dol the di do,
He was a proud one
I tell you.

If ever you go to Dublin town
In a hundred years or so
Sniff for my personality,
Is it Vanity's vapour now?
O he was a vain one,
Fol dol the di do,
He was a vain one
I tell you.

I saw his name with a hundred others
In a book in the library,
It said he had never fully achieved
His potentiality.
O he was slothful,
Fol dol the di do,
He was slothful
I tell you.

He knew that posterity has no use
For anything but the soul,
The lines that speak the passionate heart,
The spirit that lives alone.
O he was a lone one,
Fol dol the di do,
Yet he lived happily
I tell you.

Patrick Kavanagh
(1904–1967)

TO THE FOUR COURTS, PLEASE

The driver rubbed at his nettly chin
With a huge loose forefinger, crooked and black;
And his wobbly violet lips sucked in,
And puffed out again and hung down slack:
A black fang shone through his lop-sided smile,
In his little pouched eye flickered years of guile.

And the horse, poor beast! It was ribbed and forked;
And its ears hung down, and its eyes were old;
And its knees were knuckly; and, as we talked,
It swung the stiff neck that could scarcely hold
Its big skinny head up — then I stepped in,
And the driver climbed to his seat with a grin.

God help the horse, and the driver too!
And the people and beasts who have never a friend!
For the driver easily might have been you,
And the horse be me by a different end!
And nobody knows how their days will cease!
And the poor, when they're old, have little of peace!

James Stephens
(c. 1882–1950)

SAID HANRAHAN

'We'll all be rooned,' said Hanrahan,
  In accents most forlorn,
Outside the church, ere Mass began,
  One frosty Sunday morn.

The congregation stood about,
  Coat-collars to the ears,
And talked of stock, and crops, and drought,
  As it had done for years.

'It's lookin' crook,' said Daniel Croke;
  'Bedad, it's cruke, me lad,
For never since the banks went broke
  Has seasons been so bad.'

'It's dry, all right,' said young O'Neil,
   With which astute remark
He squatted down upon his heel
   And chewed a piece of bark.

And so around the chorus ran
   'It's keepin' dry, no doubt.'
'We'll all be rooned,' said Hanrahan,
   'Before the year is out.

'The crops are done; ye'll have your work
   To save one bag of grain;
From here way out to Back-o'-Bourke
   They're singin' out for rain.

'They're singin' out for rain,' he said,
   'And all the tanks are dry.'
The congregation scratched its head,
   And gazed around the sky.

'There won't be grass, in any case,
   Enough to feed an ass;
There's not a blade on Casey's place
   As I came down to Mass.'

'If rain don't come this month,' said Dan
   And cleared his throat to speak —
'We'll all be rooned,' said Hanrahan,
   'If rain don't come this week.'

A heavy silence seemed to steal
    On all at this remark;
And each man squatted on his heel,
    And chewed a piece of bark.

'We want a inch of rain, we do,'
    O'Neil observed at last;
But Croke 'mantained' we wanted two
    To put the danger past.

'If we don't get three inches, man,
    Or four to break this drought,
We'll all be rooned,' said Hanrahan,
    'Before the year is out.'

In God's good time down came the rain;
    And all the afternoon
On iron roof and windowpane
    It drummed a homely tune.

And through the night it pattered still,
    And lightsome, gladsome elves
On dripping spout and windowsill
    Kept talking to themselves.

It pelted, pelted all day long,
    A-singing at its work,
Till every heart took up the song
    Way out to Back-o'-Bourke.

And every creek a banker ran,
    And dams filled overtop;
'We'll all be rooned,' said Hanrahan,
    'If this rain doesn't stop.'

And stop it did, in God's good time;
    And spring came in to fold
A mantle o'er the hills sublime
    Of green and pink and gold.

And days went by on dancing feet,
    With harvest-hopes immense,
And laughing eyes beheld the wheat
    Nid-nodding o'er the fence.

And, oh, the smiles on every face,
    As happy lad and lass
Through grass knee-deep on Casey's place
    Went riding down to Mass.

While round the church in clothes genteel
    Discoursed the men of mark,
And each man squatted on his heel,
    And chewed his piece of bark.

'There'll be bush-fires for sure, me man,
    There will, without a doubt;
We'll all be rooned,' said Hanrahan,
    'Before the year is out.'

John O'Brien
(1879–1952)

A DROVER

To Meath of the pastures,
From wet hills by the sea,
Through Leitrim and Longford
Go my cattle and me.

I hear in the darkness
Their slipping and breathing.
I name them the bye-ways
They're to pass without heeding.

Then the wet, winding roads,
Brown bogs with black water;
And my thoughts on white ships
And the King o' Spain's daughter.

O! farmer, strong farmer!
You can spend at the fair
But your face you must turn
To your crops and your care.

And soldiers – red soldiers!
You've seen many lands;
But you walk two by two,
And by captain's commands.

O! the smell of the beasts,
The wet wind in the morn;
And the proud and hard earth
Never broken for corn;

And the crowds at the fair,
The herds loosened and blind,
Loud words and dark faces,
And the wild blood behind.

(O! strong men with your best
I would strive breast to breast
I could quiet your herds
With my words, with my words.)

I will bring you, my kine,
Where there's grass to the knee;
But you'll think of scant croppings
Harsh with salt of the sea.

                              Padraic Colum
                              (1881–1972)

THE WOMAN OF THREE COWS

Oh Woman of Three Cows, *agra!* don't let your tongue thus
    rattle!
Oh, don't be saucy, don't be stiff, because you may have
    cattle.
I have seen – and, here's my hand to you, I only say what's
    true –
A many a one with twice your stock not half so proud as
    you.

Good luck to you, don't scorn the poor, and don't be their
    despiser,
For worldly wealth soon melts away, and cheats the very
    miser,
And Death soon strips the proudest wreath from haughty
    human brows;
Then don't be stiff, and don't be proud, good Woman of
    Three Cows!

See where Momonia's heroes lie, proud Owen More's
    descendants,
'Tis they that won the glorious name, and had the grand
    attendants!
If *they* were forced to bow to Fate, as every mortal bows,
Can *you* be proud, can *you* be stiff, my Woman of Three
    Cows?

The brave sons of the Lord of Clare, they left the land to
    mourning;
Mavrone! for they were banished, with no hope of their
    returning –
Who knows in what abodes of want those youths were
    driven to house?
Yet *you* can give yourself these airs, O Woman of Three
    Cows!

Oh, think of Donnell of the Ships, the Chief whom nothing
    daunted –
See how he fell in distant Spain, unchronicled, unchanted!
He sleeps, the great O'Sullivan, where thunder cannot
    rouse –
Then ask yourself, should *you* be proud, good Woman of
    Three Cows!

O'Ruark, Maguire, those souls of fire, whose names are
    shrined in story –
Think how their high achievements once made Erin's
    highest glory –
Yet now their bones lie mouldering under weeds and cypress
    boughs,
And so, for all your pride, will yours, O Woman of Three
    Cows!

The O'Carrolls, also, famed when Fame was only for the
    boldest,
Rest in forgotten sepulchres with Erin's best and oldest;
Yet who so great as they of yore in battle or carouse?
Just think of that, and hide your head, good Woman of
    Three Cows!

Your neighbour's poor, and you, it seems, are big with vain
    ideas,
Because, *inagh!* you've got three cows – one more, I see,
    than *she* has.
That tongue of yours wags more at times than Charity
    allows,
But if you're strong, be merciful, great Woman of Three
    Cows!

Now, there you go! You still, of course, keep up your
  scornful bearing,
And I'm too poor to hinder you; but, by the cloak I'm
  wearing,
If I had but *four* cows myself, even though you were my
  spouse,
I'd thwack you well to cure your pride, my Woman of Three
  Cows!

Anonymous (17th century)
translated from the Irish by
J.C. Mangan
(1803–1849)

79

THE WAYFARER

Written the night before his execution

The beauty of the world hath made me sad,
This beauty that will pass;
Sometimes my heart hath shaken with great joy
To see a leaping squirrel in a tree,
Or a red ladybird upon a stalk,
Or little rabbits in a field at evening,
Lit by a slanting sun,
Or some green hill where shadows drifted by,
Some quiet hill where mountainy man hath sown
And soon would reap; near to the gate of heaven;
Or children with bare feet upon the sands
Of some ebbed sea, or playing on the streets
Of little towns in Connacht,
Things young and happy.
And then my heart hath told me:
These will pass,
Will pass and change, will die and be no more,
Things bright and green, things young and happy;
And I have gone upon my way
Sorrowful.

Patrick Pearse
(1879–1916)

THE WINDING BANKS OF ERNE:

or

THE EMIGRANT'S ADIEU TO BALLYSHANNON

A Local Ballad

Adieu to Ballyshannon! where I was bred and born;
Go where I may, I'll think of you, as sure as night and morn,
The kindly spot, the friendly town, where everyone is known,
And not a face in all the place but partly seems my own;
There's not a house or window, there's not a field or hill,
But, east or west, in foreign lands, I'll recollect them still.
I leave my warm heart with you, though my back I'm forced
 to turn –
So adieu to Ballyshannon, and the winding banks of Erne!

No more on pleasant evenings we'll saunter down the Mall,
When the trout is rising to the fly, the salmon to the fall.
The boat comes straining on her net, and heavily she creeps,
Cast off, cast off! – she feels the oars, and to her berth she sweeps;
Now fore and aft keep hauling, and gathering up the clue,
Till a silver wave of salmon rolls in among the crew.
Then they may sit, with pipes a-lit, and many a joke and 'yarn'; –
Adieu to Ballyshannon, and the winding banks of Erne!

The music of the waterfall, the mirror of the tide,
When all the green-hill'd harbour is full from side to side –
From Portnasun to Bulliebawns, and round the Abbey Bay,
From rocky Inis Saimer to Coolnargit sandhills grey;
While far upon the southern line, to guard it like a wall,
The Leitrim mountains, clothed in blue, gaze calmly over all,
And watch the ship sail up or down, the red flag at her stern; –
Adieu to these, adieu to all the winding banks of Erne!

Farewell to you, Kildoney lads, and them that pull an oar,
A lugsail set, or haul a net, from the Point to Mullaghmore;
From Killybegs to bold Slieve League, that ocean-mountain steep,
Six hundred yards in air aloft, six hundred in the deep;
From Dooran to the Fairy Bridge, and round by Tullen strand,
Level and long, and white with waves, where gull and curlew
    stand; –
Head out to sea when on your lee the breakers you discern! –
Adieu to all the billowy coast, and winding banks of Erne!

Farewell Coolmore, – Bundoran! and your summer crowds
    that run
From inland homes to see with joy th' Atlantic-setting sun;

To breathe the buoyant salted air, and sport among the waves;
To gather shells on sandy beach, and tempt the gloomy caves;
To watch the flowing, ebbing tide, the boats, the crabs, the fish;
Young men and maids to meet and smile, and form a tender wish;
The sick and old in search of health, for all things have their turn—
And I must quit my native shore, and the winding banks of Erne!

Farewell to every white cascade from the harbour to Belleek,
And every pool where fins may rest, and ivy-shaded creek;
The sloping fields, the lofty rocks, where ash and holly grow,
The one split yew tree gazing on the curving flood below;
The Lough, that winds through islands under Turaw mountain
     green;
And Castle Caldwell's stretching woods, with tranquil bays
     between;
And Breesie Hill, and many a pond among the heath and fern, –
For I must say adieu – adieu to the winding banks of Erne!

The thrush will call through Camlin groves the live-long
     summer day;
The waters run by mossy cliff, and bank with wild flowers gay;
The girls will bring their work and sing beneath a twisted thorn,
Or stray with sweethearts down the path among the growing
     corn;
Along the river side they go, where I have often been, –
O, never shall I see again the days that I have seen!
A thousand chances are to one I never may return, –
Adieu to Ballyshannon, and the winding banks of Erne!

Adieu to evening dances, when merry neighbours meet,
And the fiddle says to boys and girls, 'Get up and shake your feet!'

To 'shanachus' and wise old talk of Erin's days gone by –
Who trench'd the rath on such a hill, and where the bones may lie
Of saint, or king, or warrior chief; with tales of fairy power,
And tender ditties sweetly sung to pass the twilight hour.
The mournful song of exile is now for me to learn –
Adieu, my dear companions on the winding banks of Erne!

Now measure from the Commons down to each end of the Purt,
Round the Abbey, Moy, and Knather, – I wish no one any hurt;
The Main Street, Back Street, College Lane, the Mall, and
    Portnasun,
If any foes of mine are there, I pardon every one.
I hope that man and womankind will do the same by me;
For my heart is sore and heavy at voyaging the sea.
My loving friends I'll bear in mind, and often fondly turn
To think of Ballyshannon, and the winding banks of Erne.

If ever I'm a money'd man, I mean, please God, to cast
My golden anchor in the place where youthful years were pass'd;
Though heads that now are black and brown must meanwhile
    gather grey,
New faces rise by every hearth, and old ones drop away –
Yet dearer still that Irish hill than all the world beside;
It's home, sweet home, where'er I roam, through lands and
    waters wide.
And if the Lord allows me, I surely will return
To my native Ballyshannon, and the winding banks of Erne.

William Allingham
(1824 – 1889)

84

THE ROADS AROUND RATHOE

The old County Carlow gentleman in New York

My son has brought me over to end my many days
Amidst his wealth an' comfortin's that meet my
    worn-out gaze.
I'm sure the boy manes well enough an' the wife's a
    treasure, too;
She calls me 'Pop' an' 'Popakins', an' smiles with eyes of blue
Upon me every notion, an' sure I've many quare;
She roared at my describin' the scenes 'round Carlow Fair.
Although they do their best to make me feel at home
    an' safe,
I'd rather tread this moment the brown of autumn lafe
That makes a thickened carpet along where streamlets
    flow –
I'd rather be a-strollin' on the roads around Rathoe!

There were forty friends last evenin' received by the son
    an' wife;
I never felt so out of place in all my mortal life;
Oh, glory be – the style o' them would make your head
    to ache:
I wonder if the young ones, now, is anythin' but fake.
The way their mouths was painted an' their eyebrows
    straked with black,
They had no hair upon their heads to hould a comb or rack;
Some o' thim you couldn't tell no difference from the boys.
An' they kicked up holy ructions – oh, they made an
    awful noise.
If this is called amusement it's something I'll forego –
I'd rather watch them wrastlin' on the roads around
    Rathoe!

They have their breakfasts in their beds an' they call me
    dinner lunch;
If they're struck with an idea, sure they says: 'We've got
    a hunch';
They never seem to walk at all – it's ayther car or 'plane.
I sometimes think they've go no sinse, they seem to me
    insane,
They gamble, sure, from morn till night, an' never count
    the loss,
Tho' none o' them could take a hand at honest pitch
    an' toss!
An' as for cards: such games they play, it bates – och,
    man alive,
You may as well ax for heaven as a game of th' ould
    Twenty-five;
They can't address you dacint; if they're friendly they
    say 'Bo!'
Ah, the spakin's very diff'rent on the roads around Rathoe!

Val Vousden
(?–1951)

86

THE OULD ORANGE FLUTE

In the County Tyrone, near the town of Dungannon,
   Where many's the ruction myself had a han' in,
Bob Williamson lived, a weaver by trade,
   And all of us thought him a stout Orange blade.
On the Twelfth of July, as it yearly did come,
   Bob played on the flute to the sound of the drum.
You may talk of your harp, your piano, or lute,
   But nothing could sound like the ould Orange flute.

But Bob the deceyver, he took us all in,
   For he married a Papish called Bridget McGinn,
Turned Papish himself, and forsook the ould cause
   That gave us our freedom, religion, and laws.
Now, the boys in the townland made comment upon it,
   And Bob had to fly to the province of Connaught.
He flew with his wife, and his fixin's to boot,
   And along with the others the ould Orange flute.

At the Chapel on Sundays to atone for past deeds,
   He said 'Paters' and 'Aves' and counted his beads,
Till, after some time, at the priest's own desire,
   He went with his ould flute to play in the choir.
He went with his ould flute to play in the Mass,
   But the instrument shivered and sighed, Oh alas!
When he blew it and fingered and made a great noise,
   The flute would play only 'The Protestant Boys'.

Bob jumped and he started and got in a splutter,
    And threw the ould flute in the Bless'd Holy Water;
He thought that this charm might bring some other
        sound.
    When he blew it again, it played 'Croppies Lie
        Down',
And all he could whistle and finger and blow,
    To play Papish music he found it no go.
'Kick the Pope', 'The Boyne Water' and such like it
        would sound,
    But one Papish squeak in it couldn't be found.

At a council of priests that was held the next day,
    They decided to banish the ould flute away;
For they couldn't knock heresy out of its head,
    And they bought Bob another to play in its stead
So the ould flute was doomed and its fate was pathetic;
    It was fastened and burned at the stake as a heretic.
While the flames roared around it, they heard a strange
        noise –
    'Twas the ould flute still whistlin' 'The Protestant
        Boys'!

Anonymous (19th century)

DAWN ON THE IRISH COAST

T'anam ó'n diabhach! but there it is –
 The dawn on the hills of Ireland!
God's angels lifting the night's black veil
 From the fair, sweet face of my sireland!
O, Ireland! isn't it grand you look –
 Like a bride in her rich adornin'!
With all the pent-up love of my heart
 I bid you the top of the mornin'!

This one short hour pays lavishly back
 For many a year of mourning;
I'd almost venture another flight,
 There's so much joy in returning –
Watching out for the hallowed shore,
 All other attractions scornin';
O, Ireland! don't you hear me shout?
 I bid you the top of the mornin'.

Ho, ho! upon Cliodhna's shelving strand
    The surges are grandly beating,
And Kerry is pushing her headlands out
    To give us the kindly greeting!
In to the shore the sea birds fly
    On pinions that know no drooping,
And out from the cliffs, with welcomes charged,
    A million of waves come trooping.

O, kindly, generous, Irish land,
    So leal and fair and loving!
No wonder the wandering Celt should think
    And dream of you in his roving.
The alien home may have gems and gold,
    Shadows may never have gloomed it;
But the heart will sigh for the absent land
    Where the love-light first illumed it.

And doesn't old Cove look charming there
    Watching the wild waves' motion,
Leaning her back up against the hills,
    And the tip of her toes in the ocean.
I wonder I don't hear Shandon's bells –
    Ah! maybe their chiming's over,
For it's many a year since I began
    The life of a western rover.

For thirty summers, *a stór mo chroidhe,*
    Those hills I now feast my eyes on
Ne'er met my vision save when they rose
    Over memory's dim horizon.
E'en so, 'twas grand and fair they seemed
    In the landscape spread before me;
But dreams are dreams, and my eyes would ope
    To see Texas' skies still o'er me.

Oh! often upon the Texan plains,
  When the day and the chase were over,
My thoughts would fly o'er the weary wave,
  And around this coastline hover;
And the prayer would rise that some future day –
  All danger and doubting scorning –
I'd help to win for my native land
  The light of young Liberty's morning!

Now fuller and truer the shoreline shows –
  Was ever a scene so splendid?
I feel the breath of the Munster breeze,
  Thank God that my exile's ended!
Old scenes, old songs, old friends again,
  The vale and the cot I was born in –
O, Ireland! up from my heart of hearts
  I bid you the top of the mornin'!

John Locke
(1847–1889)

91

TANGMALANGALOO

The bishop sat in lordly state and purple cap sublime,
And galvanized the old bush church at Confirmation time;
And all the kids were mustered up from fifty miles around,
With Sunday clothes, and staring eyes, and ignorance
    profound.
Now was it fate, or was it grace, whereby they yarded too
An overgrown two-storey lad from Tangmalangaloo?

A hefty son of virgin soil, where nature has her fling,
And grows the trefoil three feet high and mats it in
    the spring;
Where mighty hills uplift their heads to pierce the
    welkin's rim,
And trees sprout up a hundred feet before they shoot a limb;
There everything is big and grand, and men are giants too –
But Christian Knowledge wilts, alas, at Tangmalangaloo.

The bishop summed the youngsters up, as bishops only can;
He cast a searching glance around, then fixed upon his man.
But glum and dumb and undismayed through every bout
    he sat;
He seemed to think that he was there, but wasn't sure
    of that.
The bishop gave a scornful look, as bishops sometimes do,
And glared right through the pagan in from
    Tangmalangaloo.

'Come, tell me, boy,' his lordship said in crushing
    tones severe,
'Come, tell me why is Christmas Day the greatest of
    the year?
How is it that around the world we celebrate that day
And send a name upon a card to those who're far away?
Why is it wandering ones return with smiles and
    greetings, too?'
A squall of knowledge hit the lad from Tangmalangaloo.

He gave a lurch which set a-shake the vases on the shelf,
He knocked the benches all askew, up-ending of himself.
And oh, how pleased his lordship was, and how he smiled
    to say,
'That's good, my boy. Come, tell me now; and what is
    Christmas Day?'
The ready answer bared a fact no bishop ever knew —
'It's the day before the races out at Tangmalangaloo.'

John O'Brien
(1879–1952)

GOUGANE BARRA

There is a green island in lone Gougane Barra,
Where Allua of songs rushes forth as an arrow;
In deep-valleyed Desmond – a thousand wild fountains
Come down to that lake from their home in the mountains.
There grows the wild ash, and a time-stricken willow
Looks chidingly down on the mirth of the billow;
As, like some gay child, that sad monitor scorning,
It lightly laughs back to the laugh of the morning!

And its zone of dark hills – oh! to see them all bright'ning
When the tempest flings out its red banner of lightning,
And the waters rush down, 'mid the thunder's deep rattle,
Like the clans from the hills at the voice of the battle;
And brightly the fire-crested billows are gleaming,
And wildly from Mullach the eagles are screaming:
Oh! where is the dwelling in valley, or highland,
So meet for a bard as this lone little island?

How oft when the summer sun rested on Clara,
And lit the dark heath on the hills of Ivéra,
Have I sought thee, sweet spot, from my home by the ocean,
And trod all thy wilds with a minstrel's devotion,
And thought of thy bards, when assembling together,
In the cleft of thy rocks, or the depth of thy heather;
They fled from the Saxon's dark bondage and slaughter,
And waked their last song by the rush of thy water.

High sons of the lyre, oh! how proud was the feeling,
To think while alone through that solitude stealing,
Though loftier minstrels green Erin can number,
I only awoke your wild harp from its slumber,
And mingled once more with the voice of those fountains
The songs' even echo forgot on her mountains;
And gleaned each grey legend, that darkly was sleeping
Where the mist and the rain o'er their beauty were creeping.

94

Least bard of the hills! were it mine to inherit
The fire of thy harp, and the wing of thy spirit,
With the wrongs which like thee to our country has bound me,
Did your mantle of song fling its radiance around me:
Still, still in those wilds might young liberty rally,
And send her strong shout over mountain and valley,
The star of the West might yet rise in its glory,
And the land that was darkest be brightest in story.

I, too, shall be gone – but my name shall be spoken,
When Erin awakes, and her fetters are broken;
Some minstrel will come in the summer eve's gleaming,
When freedom's young light on his spirit is beaming,
And bend o'er my grave with a tear of emotion,
Where calm Abhann Buidhe seeks the kisses of ocean,
Or plant a wild wreath from the banks of that river
O'er the heart, and the harp, that are sleeping for ever.

J.J. Callanan
(1795–1829)

95

THE WAY WE TELL A STORY

Says I to him, I says, says I,
Says I to him, I says,
The thing, says I, I says to him,
Is just, says I, this ways.
I hev', says I, a gret respeck
For you and for your breed,
And onything I cud, I says,
I'd do, I wud indeed.
I don't know any man, I says,
I'd do it for, says I,
As fast, I says, as for yoursel',
That's tellin' ye no lie.
There's nought, says I, I wudn't
do
To plase your feyther's son,
But this, I says, ye see, says I,
I says, it can't be done.

Pat McCarty
(*c.* 1851–1931)

1691

A BALLAD OF ATHLONE (2ND SIEGE)

or

HOW THEY BROKE DOWN THE BRIDGE

Does any man dream that a Gael can fear? –
 Of a thousand deeds let him learn but one!
The Shannon swept onward broad and clear,
 Between the leaguers and broad Athlone.

'Break down the bridge!' – Six warriors rushed
 Through the storm of shot and the storm of shell:
With late but certain victory flushed
 The grim Dutch gunners eyed them well.

They wrench'd at the planks 'mid a hail of fire:
 They fell in death, their work half done:
The bridge stood fast; and nigh and nigher
 The foe swarmed darkly, densely on.

'O, who for Erin will strike a stroke?
 Who hurl yon planks where the waters roar?'
Six warriors forth from their comrades broke,
 And flung them upon that bridge once more.

Again at the rocking planks they dashed;
 And four dropped dead; and two remained:
The huge beams groaned, and the arch down-crashed; –
 Two stalwart swimmers the margin gained.

St Ruth in his stirrups stood up, and cried,
 'I have seen no deed like that in France!'
With a toss of his head, Sarsfield replied,
 'They had luck, the dogs! 'Twas a merry chance!'

O many a year upon Shannon's side
    They sang upon moor and they sang upon heath
Of the twain that breasted that raging tide,
    And the ten that shook bloody hands with Death!

Aubrey De Vere
(1814–1902)

How they kept the Bridge at Athlone.

THE MAN FROM GOD-KNOWS-WHERE

Into our townlan', on a night of snow,
Rode a man from God-knows-where;
None of us bade him stay or go,
Nor deemed him friend, nor damned him foe.
But we stabled his big roan mare;
For in our townlan' we're decent folk,
And if he didn't speak, why none of us spoke,
And we sat till the fire burned low.

We're a civil sort in our wee place,
So we made the circle wide
Round Andy Lemon's cheerful blaze,
And wished the man his length of days,
And a good end to his ride.
He smiled in under his slouchy hat —
Says he: 'There's a bit of a joke in that,
For we ride different ways.'

The whiles we smoked we watched him stare
From his seat fornenst the glow.
I nudged Joe Moore: 'You wouldn't dare
To ask him, who he's for meeting there,
And how far he has got to go.'
And Joe wouldn't dare, nor Wully Scott,
And he took no drink — neither cold nor hot —
This man from God-knows-where.

It was closin' time, an' late forbye,
When us ones braved the air —
I never saw worse (may I live or die)
Than the sleet that night, an' I says, says I:
'You'll find he's for stopping there.'
But at screek o' day, through the gable pane,
I watched him spur in the peltin' rain,
And I juked from his rovin' eye.

Two winters more, then the Trouble Year,
When the best that a man can feel
Was the pike he kept in hidin's near,
Till the blood o' hate an' the blood o' fear
Would be redder nor rust on the steel.
Us ones quiet from mindin' the farms,
Let them take what we gave wi' the weight o' our arms,
From Saintfield to Kilkeel.

In the time o' the Hurry, we had no lead —
We all of us fought with the rest —
An' if e'er a one shook like a tremblin' reed,
None of us gave neither hint nor heed.
Nor ever even'd we'd guessed.
We men of the North had a word to say,
An' we said it then, in our own dour way,
An' we spoke as we thought was best.

All Ulster over, the weemen cried
For the stan'in' crops on the lan' –
Many's the sweetheart an' many's the bride
Would liefer ha' gone till where He died,
And ha' mourned her lone by her man.
But us ones weathered the thick of it,
And we used to dander along and sit,
In Andy's, side by side.

What with discorse goin' to and fro,
The night would be wearin' thin,
Yet never so late when we rose to go
But someone would say: 'Do ye min' thon snow,
An' the man who came wanderin' in?'
And we be to fall to the talk again,
If by any chance he was One o' Them –
The man who went like the win'.

Well 'twas gettin' on past the heat o' the year
When I rode to Newtown fair;
I sold as I could (the dealers were near –
Only three pounds eight for the Innish steer,
An' nothin' at all for the mare!)
I met M'Kee in the throng o' the street,
Says he: 'The grass has grown under our feet
Since they hanged young Warwick here.'

And he told me that Boney had promised help
To a man in Dublin town.
Says he: 'If you've laid the pike on the shelf,
Ye'd better go home hot-fut by yourself,
An' once more take it down.'
So by Comber road I trotted the grey
And never cut corn until Killyleagh
Stood plain on the rising groun'.

For a wheen o' days we sat waitin' the word
To rise and go at it like men.
But no French ships sailed into Cloughey Bay,
And we heard the black news on a harvest day
That the cause was lost again;
And Joey and me, and Wully Boy Scott,
We agreed to ourselves we'd as lief as not
Ha' been found in the thick o' the slain.

By Downpatrick gaol I was bound to fare
On a day I'll remember, feth,
For when I came to the prison square
The people were waitin' in hundreds there,
An' you wouldn't hear stir nor breath!
For the sodgers were standing, grim an' tall,
Round a scaffold built there fornent the wall,
An' a man stepped out for death!

I was brave an' near to the edge of the throng,
Yet I knowed the face again.
An' I knowed the set, an' I knowed the walk
An' the sound of his strange up-country talk,
For he spoke out right an' plain.
Then he bowed his head to the swinging rope,
Whiles I said, 'Please God' to his dying hope,
And 'Amen' to his dying prayer,
That the Wrong would cease and the Right prevail,
For the man that they hanged at Downpatrick gaol
Was the Man from GOD-KNOWS-WHERE!

Florence M. Wilson
(?–1946)

THE SACK OF BALTIMORE

AD 1631

The summer sun is falling soft on Carbery's hundred isles —
The summer sun is gleaming still through Gabriel's rough defiles —
Old Inisherkin's crumbled fane looks like a moulting bird;
And in a calm and sleepy swell the ocean tide is heard;
The hookers lie upon the beach; the children cease their play;
The gossips leave the little inn; the households kneel to pray —
And full of love, and peace, and rest — its daily labour o'er —
Upon that cosy creek there lay the town of Baltimore.

A deeper rest, a starry trance, has come with midnight there;
No sound, except that throbbing wave, in earth, or sea, or air.
The massive capes, and ruined towers, seemed conscious of
    the calm;
The fibrous sod and stunted trees are breathing heavy balm.
So still the night, these two long barques, round Dunashad
    that glide,
Must trust their oars — methinks not few — against the
    ebbing tide —
Oh! some sweet mission of true love should urge them to
    the shore —
They bring some lover to his bride, who sighs in Baltimore!

All, all asleep within each roof along that rocky street,
And these must be the lover's friends with gently gliding feet —
A stifled gasp! a dreamy noise! 'the roof is in a flame!'
From out their beds, and to their doors, rush maid, and sire,
    and dame —
And meet, upon the threshold stone, the gleaming sabres' fall,
And o'er each black and bearded face the white or crimson
    shawl —
The yell of 'Allah' breaks above the prayer, and shriek and roar —
Oh, blessed God! the Algerine is lord of Baltimore!

Then flung the youth his naked hand against the shearing sword;
Then sprung the mother on the brand with which her son
   was gored;
Then sunk the grandsire on the floor, his grandbabes
   clutching wild;
Then fled the maiden moaning faint and nestled with the child:
But see, yon pirate strangled lies, and crushed with splashing heel,
While o'er him, in an Irish hand, there sweeps his Syrian steel,
Though virtue sink, and courage fail, and misers yield their store,
There's one hearth well avengèd in the sack of Baltimore!

Midsummer morn, in woodland nigh, the birds begin to sing –
They see not now the milking maids – deserted is the spring!
Midsummer day – this gallant rides from distant Bandon's town –
These hookers crossed from stormy Schull, that skiff
   from Affadown;
They only found the smoking walls, with neighbours' blood
   besprint,
And on the strewed and trampled beach awhile they wildly went –
Then dashed to sea, and passed Cape Clere, and saw five
   leagues before
The pirate galleys vanishing, that ravaged Baltimore.

Oh! some must tug the galleys o'er, and some must tend
   the steed –
This boy will bear a Sheik's chibouk, and that a Bey's jerreed.
Oh! some are for the arsenals, by beauteous Dardanelles;
And some are in the caravan to Mecca's sandy dells.
The maid that Bandon gallant sought is chosen for the Dey
She's safe – he's dead – she stabbed him in the midst of his serai;
And, when to die a death of fire that noble maid they bore,
She only smiled – O'Driscoll's child – she thought of Baltimore.

'Tis two long years since sunk the town beneath that bloody band,
And now amid its trampled hearths a larger concourse stand,
Where, high upon a gallows tree, a yelling wretch is seen –
'Tis Hackett of Dungarvan – he who steered the Algerine!
He fell amid a sullen shout, with scarce a passing prayer,
For he had slain the kith and kin of many a hundred there –
Some muttered of MacMurchaidh, who brought the
   Norman o'er –
Some cursed him with Iscariot, that day in Baltimore.

Thomas Davis
(1814–1845)

SEPTEMBER 1913

What need you, being come to sense,
But fumble in a greasy till
And add the halfpence to the pence
And prayer to shivering prayer, until
You have dried the marrow from the bone?
For men were born to pray and save:
Romantic Ireland's dead and gone,
It's with O'Leary in the grave.

Yet they were of a different kind,
The names that stilled your childish play,
They have gone about the world like wind,
But little time had they to pray
For whom the hangman's rope was spun,
And what, God help us, could they save?
Romantic Ireland's dead and gone,
It's with O'Leary in the grave.

Was it for this the wild geese spread
The grey wing upon every tide;
For this that all that blood was shed,
For this Edward Fitzgerald died,
And Robert Emmet and Wolfe Tone,
All that delirium of the brave?
Romantic Ireland's dead and gone,
It's with O'Leary in the grave.

Yet could we turn the years again,
And call those exiles as they were
In all their loneliness and pain,
You'd cry, 'Some woman's yellow hair
Has maddened every mother's son':
They weighed so lightly what they gave.
But let them be, they're dead and gone,
They're with O'Leary in the grave.

W.B. Yeats
(1865–1939)

FONTENOY

Thrice at the huts of Fontenoy, the English column failed,
And, twice, the lines of Saint Antoine, the Dutch in vain assailed;
For town and slope were filled with fort, and flanking battery,
And well they swept the English ranks and Dutch auxiliary.
As vainly, through De Barri's wood, the British soldiers burst,
The French artillery drove them back diminished and dispersed.
The bloody Duke of Cumberland beheld with anxious eye,
And ordered up his last reserve, his latest chance to try.
On Fontenoy, on Fontenoy, how fast his general's ride!
And mustering come his chosen troops, like clouds at eventide.

Six thousand English veterans in stately column tread,
Their cannon blaze in front and flank — Lord Hay is at their head;
Steady they step adown the slope — steady they climb the hill;
Steady they load, — steady they fire, moving right onward still,
Betwixt the wood and Fontenoy, as through a furnace blast,
Through rampart, trench and palisade, and bullets
    showering fast;
And on the open plain above they rose and kept their course,
With ready fire and grim resolve that mocked at hostile force:
Past Fontenoy, past Fontenoy, while thinner grew their ranks —
They break, as broke the Zuyder Zee through Holland's
    ocean banks.

More idly than the summer flies, French tirailleurs rush round;
As stubble to the lava tide, French squadrons strew the ground,
Bombshell and grape and round-shot tore, still on they marched
    and fired —
Fast from each volley grenadier and voltigeur retired.
'Push on, my household cavalry!' King Louis madly cried;
To death they rush, but rude their shock — not unavenged
    they died.

On through the camp the column trod – King Louis turns his rein.
'Not yet, my liege,' Saxe interposed, 'the Irish troops remain';
And Fontenoy, famed Fontenoy, had been a Waterloo
Were not these exiles ready then, fresh, vehement and true.

'Lord Clare,' he says, 'you have your wish, there are your
   Saxon foes!'
The Marshal almost smiles to see, so furiously he goes!
How fierce the look these exiles wear, who're wont to be so gay,
The treasured wrongs of fifty years are in their hearts today –
The treaty broken, e'er the ink wherewith 'twas writ could dry,
Their plundered homes, their ruined shrines, their women's
   parting cry,
Their priesthood, hunted down like wolves, their country
   overthrown –
Each looks as if revenge for all were staked on him alone.
On Fontenoy! on Fontenoy! nor ever yet elsewhere,
Rushed on to fight a nobler band than these proud exiles were.

O'Brien's voice is hoarse with joy, as, halting, he commands,
'Fix bay'nets' – 'Charge!' – Like mountain storm, rush on these
   fiery bands!
Thin is the English column now, and faint their volleys grow,
Yet, must'ring all the strength they have, they make a
   gallant show.
They dress their ranks upon the hill to face that battle wind –
Their bayonets the breaker's foam, like rocks the men behind.
One volley crashes from their line, when, through the
   surging smoke,
With empty guns clutched in their hands the headlong Irish broke.
On Fontenoy, on Fontenoy, hark to that fierce Huzza!
'Revenge! remember Limerick! dash down the Sassanagh!'

Like lions leaping at a fold, when mad with hunger's pang,
Right up against the English line, the Irish exiles sprang:

Bright was their steel, 'tis bloody now, their guns are filled
  with gore;
Through shattered ranks, and severed files, and trampled flags
  they tore;
The English strove with desperate strength, paused, rallied,
  staggered, fled –
The green hillside is matted close with dying and with dead;
Across the plain and far away passed on that hideous wrack,
While cavalier and fantassin dash in upon their track.
On Fontenoy! on Fontenoy! like eagles in the sun,
With bloody plumes the Irish stand – the field is fought and won!

Thomas Davis
(1814–1845)

ON BEHALF OF SOME IRISHMEN NOT FOLLOWERS OF TRADITION

They call us aliens, we are told,
Because our wayward visions stray
From that dim banner they unfold,
The dreams of worn-out yesterday.
The sum of all the past is theirs,
The creeds, the deeds, the fame, the name,
Whose death-created glory flares
And dims the spark of living flame.
They weave the necromancer's spell,
And burst the graves where martyrs slept,
Their ancient story to retell,
Renewing tears the dead have wept.
And they would have us join their dirge,
This worship of an extinct fire
In which they drift beyond the verge
Where races all outworn expire.
The worship of the dead is not
A worship that our hearts allow,
Though every famous shade were wrought
With woven thorns above the brow.
We fling our answer back in scorn:
'We are less children of this clime
Than of some nation yet unborn
Or empire in the womb of time.
We hold the Ireland in the heart
More than the land our eyes have seen,
And love the goal for which we start
More than the tale of what has been.'

The generations as they rise
May live the life men lived before,
Still hold the thought once held as wise,
Go in and out by the same door.
We leave the easy peace it brings:
The few we are shall still unite
In fealty to unseen kings
Or unimaginable light.
We would no Irish sign efface,
But yet our lips would gladlier hail
The firstborn of the Coming Race
Than the last splendour of the Gael.
No blazoned banner we unfold –
One charge alone we give to youth,
Against the sceptred myth to hold
The golden heresy of truth.

George Russell (AE)
(1867–1935)

BALLAD TO A TRADITIONAL REFRAIN

Red brick in the suburbs, white horse on the wall,
Eyetalian marble in the City Hall:
O stranger from England, why stand so aghast?
May the Lord in His mercy be kind to Belfast.

This jewel that houses our hopes and our fears
Was knocked up from the swamp in the last hundred years
But the last shall be first and the first shall be last:
May the Lord in His mercy be kind to Belfast.

We swore by King William there'd never be seen
An All-Irish Parliament at College Green,
So at Stormont we're nailing the flag to the mast:
May the Lord in His mercy be kind to Belfast.

O the bricks they will bleed and the rain it will weep,
And the damp Lagan fog lull the city to sleep;
It's to hell with the future and live on the past:
May the Lord in His mercy be kind to Belfast.

Maurice James Craig
(1919–   )

Barber : " Much off, sir ? "
Viscount Craigavon : " Not an inch ! "

ECCLESIASTES

God, you could grow to love it, God-fearing, God-
    chosen purist little puritan that,
for all your wiles and smiles, you are (the
    dank churches, the empty streets,
the shipyard silence, the tied-up swings) and
    shelter your cold heart from the heat
of the world, from woman-inquisition, from the
    bright eyes of children. Yes, you could
wear black, drink water, nourish a fierce zeal
    with locusts and wild honey, and not
feel called upon to understand and forgive
    but only to speak with a bleak
afflatus, and love the January rains when they
    darken the dark doors and sink hard
into the Antrim hills, the bog meadows, the heaped
    graves of your fathers. Bury that red
bandana and stick, that banjo. This is your
    country, close one eye and be king.
Your people await you, their heavy washing
    flaps for you in the housing estates –
a credulous people. God, you could do it, God
    help you, stand on a corner stiff
with rhetoric, promising nothing under the sun.

Derek Mahon
(1941–)

from THE BALLAD OF READING GAOL

He did not wear his scarlet coat,
   For blood and wine are red,
And blood and wine were on his hands
   When they found him with the dead,
The poor dead woman whom he loved,
   And murdered in her bed.

He walked amongst the Trial Men
   In a suit of shabby grey;
A cricket cap was on his head,
   And his step seemed light and gay;
But I never saw a man who looked
   So wistfully at the day.

I never saw a man who looked
   With such a wistful eye
Upon that little tent of blue
   Which prisoners call the sky,
And at every drifting cloud that went
   With sails of silver by.

I walked, with other souls in pain,
   Within another ring,
And was wondering if the man had done
   A great or little thing,
When a voice behind me whispered low,
   'That fellow's got to swing'. . .

There is no chapel on the day
    On which they hang a man:
The Chaplain's heart is far too sick,
    Or his face is far too wan,
Or there is that written in his eyes
    Which none should look upon.

So they kept us close till nigh on noon,
    And then they rang the bell,
And the warders with their jingling keys
    Opened each listening cell,
And down the iron stair we tramped,
    Each from his separate hell.

Out into God's sweet air we went,
    But not in wonted way,
For this man's face was white with fear,
    And that man's face was grey,
And I never saw sad men who looked
    So wistfully at the day.

I never saw sad men who looked
    With such a wistful eye
Upon that little tent of blue
    We prisoners called the sky,
And at every happy cloud that passed
    In such strange freedom by.

The warders strutted up and down,
    And watched their herd of brutes,
Their uniforms were spick and span,
    And they wore their Sunday suits,
But we knew the work they had been at,
    By the quicklime on their boots.

For where a grave had opened wide,
    There was no grave at all:
Only a stretch of mud and sand
    By the hideous prison wall,
And a little heap of burning lime,
    That the man should have his pall.

For three long years they will not sow
    Or root or seedling there:
For three long years the unblessed spot
    Will sterile be and bare,
And look upon the wondering sky
    With unreproachful stare.

They think a murderer's heart would taint
    Each simple seed they sow.
It is not true! God's kindly earth
    Is kindlier than men know,
And the red rose would but blow more red,
    The white rose whiter blow.

Oscar Wilde
(1854–1900)

TO MY DAUGHTER BETTY, THE GIFT OF GOD

In the field, before Guillemont, Somme, September 4, 1916

In wiser days, my darling rosebud, blown
To beauty proud as was your mother's prime,
In that desired, delayed, incredible time,
You'll ask why I abandoned you, my own,
And the dear heart that was your baby throne,
To dice with death. And, oh! they'll give you rhyme
And reason: some will call the thing sublime,
And some decry it in a knowing tone.
So here, while the mad guns curse overhead,
And tired men sigh, with mud for couch and floor,
Know that we fools, now with the foolish dead,
Died not for flag, nor King, nor Emperor,
But for a dream, born in a herdsman's shed,
And for the secret Scripture of the poor.

Thomas Kettle
(1880–1916)

120

HEROES

First published in 1912, the year of the Titanic *disaster*

What is a man? Not ours to ask,
Not ours to make reply.
But from Southampton to the Clyde
Can Britain testify –
That they are men and more than men
Who know the way to die.

The little blue fox has seen it break apart from the riven floe,
The little blue fox of the Arctic waste that seeks its food in the
　snow;
On gale-gored beach and wave-washed cliff the bear has seen it
　reel,
The polar bear as it left its lair to hunt for the frozen seal.
The lone moose bull on some outcast cape has wondered to see it
　pass,
As it shuffled the snow off its feeding grounds and sought for the
　meagre grass.

The sealer scurried from out its track, and the frightened whaler
　fled,
For the derelict berg on the fishing seas is a thing of fear and dread.
'Twas battered and worn by icy waves and swept by their
　madd'ning wrath,
And the Northern Lights came out at night to glare on its lonely
　path.
But ever and on 'neath the dusk and dawn to the southern seas it
　bore,
With the lean locked lands of the north astern and the trackless
　seas before.

Proudly she swung from the crowded pier, as the mooring chains
  ran free,
Virgin pure from the Belfast docks, to the olden trail of the sea.
As the music swelled from the fading beach, the pounding screws
  replied,
And the grey, lank waves went gliding by, an arm's reach
  overside.
Alas! for the joy of the lover and maid, alas! for the children gay —
The little blue fox on the Arctic waste is safer by far than they.

West! and the English fields grew dim, and the coastwise lights
  shone clear.
Say, did they laugh on the crowded decks, and the doom so very
  near?
West! and the coastwise lights gave out, and the stars of heaven
  shone,
And the sailor watched through the midnight hour, aloof, apart,
  alone.

South! 'neath the sinister polar star the death-bearing berg went
  forth.
Oh! they who sail on herded seas should dread the Doom of the
  North.
May heaven pity the sailor man, when the Northern Doom's
  abroad,
For the ship is built by the human hand, the berg by the hand of
  God.
The stars looked down from the lonely sky — as they looked on the
  polar snow
Where the bear had eaten the little blue fox it killed by the Arctic
  floe.

Say, was the joke in the stateroom heard, the laugh on the
maiden's lips?
Lord of the waves! have pity on men who go down to the sea in
ships.
Say, did the grimy stoker smile in the heat of the furnace breath?
We do not know, but this we know, he laughed in the face of
Death.
Say, did the lover hurry and fret to come to his sweetheart's side?
We only know, when the davits swung, he gallantly stood aside.
And some there were, whose life and work was much
misunderstood,
But in the hour that tried their souls, we know their death was
good.
And greater by far than deeds of war or right or a grand mistake
Is a life that is given in sacrifice for a child or a woman's sake.

What is a man? Not ours to ask,
Nor yet to make reply.
But from Southampton to the Clyde
Can Britain testify –
That they are men and more than men
Who know the way to die.

Patrick MacGill
(1891–1963)

VICTORIA-N-EDWARDIANA
*A melodramatic tragedy concocted of evergreen
favourites, odds-and-ends, bits-and-pieces and a
cast of thousands!*

It was the schooner Hesperus that sailed the wintry seas
Homeward bound from Katmandu and the heights of the
    Himalees,
With a cargo of *yellow idols,* and a skipper called *Mad
    Carew*
And a thousand *Bengal Lancers* making up the gallant crew.
They set a course for the *Inchcape Rock* with sails set fore
    and square
Crying: '*Oh to be in England now that April's there!*'
For the crew were tired and weary, and hadn't slept a wink
With water, water everywhere, nor any drop to drink.
*'Twas Friday morn when they set sail and the ocean waves
    did rage*
But *'stone walls do not a prison make, nor iron bars a cage'*
*When at last they spied a mermaid with a comb held in her
    hand*
Says Mad Carew: 'We're doomed! We never shall see
    land. . .
'Tis the curse of those green-eyed monsters that we robbed
    from Katmandu
They've nailed me once before, so I know a thing or two!'

Then up spoke *Ralph the Rover,* his voice was soft and calm
'*Boys' says he, 'Yez don't know me and none of you care a
    damn,*

*But East is East, and West is West, and never the twain shall
    meet*
So *ye Mariners of England* – you're doomed of all the fleet!'
Then he lit his pipe so calmly and tossed away the match. . .
Which settled on the dynamite that lay beneath the hatch.
'Yes boys,' says he, 'this curse is true, no wonder I perspire
I'll bet my poke within an hour this ship will be on fire.'
*Now Sam Magee was from Tennessee where the cotton
    blooms and grows*
And he was first to see the flames that there and then arose,
*'Yo-ho-ho and a bottle o' rum, and the devil has done for the
    rest!'*
Sang the sprightly Sam as he sprang to the mast and raced
    for the crow's nest.
'I am monarch of all I survey!' From up aloft he quipped
And he did a little sailor's jig – just before he slipped!
For the mast was tall and the mast was wet and the wind was
    a whetted blade. . .
Full fathoms five poor Sam lies, of his bones are coral made.

Meanwhile, below, the flames still leaped and the gunwales
    they were tinder
The fire spread out and it quickly burned the mizzen to a
    cinder,
And the boys stood on the burning deck and called out to
    the shore:
*'We could not love thee half so much, loved we not honour
    more!'*
But Honor Moore was far away, at the burial of her dad
(Corunna town was hushed that night and the troops were
    very sad)
*Not a drum was heard, not a funeral note, as his corse to the
    ramparts they carried,*
And poor Honor Moore, who loved Carew, was hoping to
    get married!

Yet still upon the *Hesperus* the crew were wild with panic:
'Let's change our luck! Rename the ship — let's christen it
    Titanic!'
Sir Ralph the Rover walked the deck, he didn't fear the ashes
*And he fixed his eye on a brighter speck and he saw the
    hopeful flashes*
'Here's the very thing we need to quell this raging fire —
An iceberg standing two miles high, a lofty snow-white
    spire!
Full steam ahead! Stand by the sheets. . . Bo'sun be not
    tardy!'
Sir Ralph then turned to Mad Carew and whispered: *'Kiss
    me, Hardy.'*
But the skipper turned his one blind eye: 'Bejaysus, you're a
    beauty —
Do you not know that England now, expects each to do his
    duty?'
Then the rush of wind, the ramp, the roar, as the decks did
    pitch and roll
When up stepped the young lad *Oliver,* a-twisting of his
    bowl
And bravely to the captain said: 'I know I am a goner. . .
But if you please, I would like some Moore. . . and I rather
    fancy Honor!'

But meanwhile on a nearby shore and a-gazing out to sea
Young Mary calling cattle home across the sands of Dee
Beheld the ice, beheld the ship, beheld the awful plight
And clapped her hands with girlish glee, crying 'Oh what a
    pretty sight!'
'No, no, alas!' her father cried, 'help must now be sought!'
*'I'll saddle up — bring forth the horse!' The horse was
    quickly brought.*
'The brigade I'll fetch,' the father vowed, 'the brave and
    bold six hundred,

And I'll save the ship, 'pon my word, before the vessel's
    sundered!'
Then he sprang to the stirrup, and Joris and he
They galloped, Dierke galloped, we galloped all three
'God speed' cried the Watch, as the gate bolts undrew
And the *Light Brigade* followed and they raced out of view,
The hounds joined in with glorious cry, the huntsman
    wound his horn,
D'ye ken John Peel at the break of day, they'll be galloping
    hard till morn!
And Young Lochinvar came out of the west, Paul Revere
    followed, *Dick Turpin, Black Bess;*
Guns to the left of them, guns to the right, half a league
    onward through the pitch black of night!
Half a league onward through the cannon smoke's whiff. . .
Till the gallant six hundred plunged over a cliff
Crying: '*Ours not to reason why,* ours but to leap and fall. . .'
Bill Brewer, Jan Stewar, Peter Gurney, Peter Davey, Dan
    Whiddon,
Harry Hawke and Uncle Tom Cobleigh and all. . . and
    Uncle Tom Cobleigh and all!
'Oh my, what fun!' Young Mary cried, 'I hope it will not
    pass!'
Alas, alas, it was too late – the ship was going fast.
Three times around went the Hesperus, three times around
    went she
And all the Bengal Lancers soon perished in the sea.
The last to go was Mad Carew, a-clinging to the rudder. . .
'Gone, gone!' Mary cried, *'and never called me Mother!'*

And now when Mary milks the cows, herself and Honor
    Moore,
They think of all the lads that drowned, 'specially poor Bill
    Brewer,

On the bonnie braes of Yarrow they sometimes sit and
   brood
And there flashes on that inward eye, that bliss of solitude,
A raging sea, the lofty ice, the flames that will not fade
A host of golden daffodils, the charge of the Light Brigade.
And down their cheeks the pearly tears often times will stray
And Mary to Miss Honor Moore is often heard to say:
'*We must go down to the sea again, to the lonely sea and the
   sky*
And all I ask is a blazing *ship* – and an iceberg two miles
   high!'

Vincent Caprani
(1934–)

ACKNOWLEDGEMENTS

Grateful acknowledgement is made to:

Angus & Robertson Publishers for permission to reprint 'Said Hanrahan' and 'Tangmalangaloo' from *Around the Boree Log* by John O'Brien, © F.A. Mechan, 1952, 1954;

Gerald Annesley for permission to reproduce an illustration by Lady Mabel Annesley;

Vincent Caprani for permission to reprint 'Victoria-n-Edwardiana';

Arthur M. Campbell for permission to reproduce a drawing;

Maurice J. Craig for permission to reprint 'Ballad to a Traditional Refrain';

J.M. Dent and Sons Ltd for permission to reproduce illustrations by Robert Gibbings from *Lovely is the Lee* and *Sweet Cork of Thee*;

Devin-Adair Publishers for permission to reprint 'Ringsend' from *Collected Poems* by Oliver St John Gogarty, © 1954 by Oliver St John Gogarty, renewed 1982;

Dundalgan Press for permission to reprint 'Wee Hughie' by Elizabeth Shane;

The Estate of Padraic Colum for permission to reprint 'An Old Woman of the Roads' and 'A Drover' by Padraic Colum;

The Estate of May Higgins for permission to reprint 'Song for the Clatter-bones' by F.R. Higgins;

The Estate of Patrick MacGill and Caliban Books for permission to reprint 'Heroes' by Patrick MacGill;

The Estate of Flann O'Brien and Granada Publishing Ltd for permission to reprint 'A Pint of Plain is Your Only Man' by Flann O'Brien;

The Estate of Moira O'Neill for permission to reprint 'Grace for Light' by Moira O'Neill;

The Estate of John Stevenson for permission to reprint 'The Way We Tell a Story' by Pat McCarty;

Gill and Macmillan Ltd for permission to reprint 'When I was Twenty-Wan' from *Ballads of a Country Boy* by Seumas MacManus;

Peter Kavanagh for permission to reprint 'If Ever You Go to Dublin Town' from *The Collected Poems of Patrick Kavanagh* by Patrick Kavanagh;

Peggy Kelly for permission to reproduce drawings from *Fifteen Years of Dublin Opinion* and *Forty Years of Dublin Opinion*;

Margaret Marshall for permission to reprint 'Me an' Me Da' by W.F. Marshall;

The Mercier Press for permission to reprint 'The Ballad of the Tinker's Daughter' from *Ballads of a Bogman* by Sigerson Clifford;

Paul Noonan for permission to reproduce a drawing;

Oxford University Press for permission to reprint 'Ecclesiastes' from *Poems 1962–1978* by Derek Mahon, © Derek Mahon, 1979;

A.D. Peters & Co., Ltd and Joan Daves for permission to reprint 'I Shall not Die' and 'Kilcash', and to quote from 'The Midnight Court' by Frank O'Connor, © 1959 by Frank O'Connor;

The Society of Authors on behalf of Iris Wise, and Macmillan Publishing Co., for permission to reprint 'A Glass of Beer', © 1918 by Macmillan Publishing Co., renewed 1946 by James Stephens, and 'To the Four Courts, Please' by James Stephens;

Waltons Musical Instrument Galleries Ltd for permission to reprint 'The Roads Around Rathoe' by Val Vousden;

Frederick Warne (Publishers) Ltd for permission to reproduce an illustration by Peter Fraser from *The Little Good People* by Kathleen Foyle;

Michael B. Yeats, Macmillan London Ltd and Macmillan Publishing Co., for permission to reprint 'September 1913', © 1916 by Macmillan Publishing Co., renewed 1944 by Bertha Georgie Yeats, 'The Lake Isle of Innisfree' and 'The Song of Wandering Aengus' by W.B. Yeats.

INDEX OF FIRST LINES AND TITLES

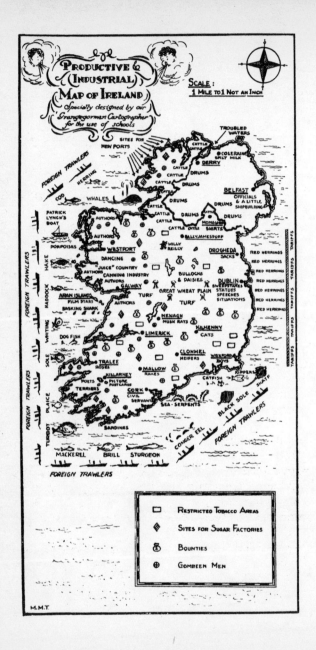